Smoking Kills

Editor: Danielle Lobban

Volume 480

independence
educational publishers

First published by
Independence Educational Publishers
The Studio, High Green
Great Shelford
Cambridge CB22 5EG
England

www.independence.co.uk

ISBN-13: 978 1 86168 940 5

Printed in Great Britain

Printed and bound by the Pureprint Group using its environmental print technology, a low-carbon, low-waste independently audited process that reduces environmental impact using 100% renewable energy, vegetable-oil-based inks and no industrial alcohol. 98% of all dry waste and 95% of press cleaning solvents are recycled. Pureprint are ISO 14001, EMAS and FSC certified and holds the Queen's Award for Enterprise: Sustainable Development.

EU Authorised Representative: Easy Access System Europe – Mustamäe tee 50, 10621 Tallinn, Estonia
Web: www.easproject.com Email: gpsr.requests@easproject.com

MIX
Paper | Supporting responsible forestry
FSC® C022913

Acknowledgements

The publisher is grateful for permission to reproduce the material in this book. While every care has been taken to trace and acknowledge copyright, the publisher tenders its apology for any accidental infringement or where copyright has proved untraceable. The publisher would be pleased to come to a suitable arrangement in any such case with the rightful owner.

The material reproduced in **issues** books is provided as an educational resource only. The views, opinions and information contained within reprinted material in **issues** books do not necessarily represent those of Independence Educational Publishers and its employees.

Although every effort has been made to ensure that website addresses are correct at time of going to press, Independence Educational Publishers cannot be held responsible for the content of any website mentioned in this book.

Images

Cover image courtesy of iStock. All other images courtesy of Freepik, Pixabay, Pexels, and Unsplash.

Additional acknowledgements

With thanks to the Independence team: Janey Hills, Elizabeth Nelson, Klaudia Sommer and Jackie Staines.

Danielle Lobban

Cambridge, July 2026

Contents

Chapter 1: The Facts

Chapter 2: Smoking in Society

Chapter 3: Quitting Smoking

Introduction

Smoking Kills is volume 480 in the **issues** series. The aim of the series is to offer current, diverse information about important issues in our world, from a UK perspective.

About *Smoking Kills*

Smoking might seem harmless at first, but the reality is very different. Tobacco kills more than 7 million people each year. *Smoking Kills* uncovers the truth about tobacco, why people start, what it does to the body, and how it affects lives. Packed with facts and strategies, this book helps you resist pressure and make healthy choices.

Our sources

Books in the **issues** series are intended to serve as educational resources, providing clear and balanced coverage of each topic.

The information in our books is comprised of facts, articles and opinions from many different sources, including:

- Newspaper reports and opinion pieces
- Website factsheets
- Magazine and journal articles
- Statistics and surveys
- Government reports
- Literature from special interest groups.

A note on critical evaluation

Because the information reprinted here is from a number of different sources, readers should bear in mind the origin of the text and whether the source is likely to have a particular bias when presenting information (or when conducting their research). It is hoped that, as you read about the many aspects of the issues explored in this book, you will critically evaluate the information presented.

It is important that you decide whether you are being presented with facts or opinions. Does the writer give a biased or unbiased report? If an opinion is being expressed, do you agree with the writer? Is there potential bias to the 'facts' or statistics behind an article?

Activities

Throughout this book, you will find a selection of assignments and activities designed to help you engage with the articles you have been reading and to explore your own opinions. Some tasks will take longer than others and there is a mixture of design, writing and research-based activities that you can complete alone or in a group.

Further research

At the end of each article we have listed its source and a website that you can visit if you would like to conduct your own research. Please remember to critically evaluate any sources that you consult and consider whether the information you are viewing is accurate and unbiased.

Issues Online

The **issues** series of books is complemented by our online resource, Issues Online.

On the Issues Online website you will find a wealth of information, covering over 75 topics, to support the PSHE and RSE curriculum.

Why Issues Online?

Researching a topic? Issues Online is the best place to start for...

Librarians

Issues Online is an essential tool for librarians: feel confident you are signposting safe, reliable, user-friendly online resources to students and teaching staff alike. We provide multi-user concurrent access, so no waiting around for another student to finish with a resource. Issues Online also provides FREE downloadable posters for your shelf/wall/table displays.

Teachers

Issues Online is an ideal resource for lesson planning, inspiring lively debate in class, and setting lessons and homework tasks.

Our accessible, engaging content helps deepen students' knowledge, promotes critical thinking, and develops independent learning skills.

Issues Online saves precious preparation time. We wade through the wealth of material on the internet to filter the best quality, most relevant and up-to-date information you need to start exploring a topic.

Our carefully selected, balanced content presents an overview and insight into each topic from a variety of sources and viewpoints.

Students

Issues Online is designed to support your studies in a broad range of topics, particularly social issues relevant to young people today.

There are thousands of articles, statistics and infographs instantly available to help you with homework, research, and assignments.

With 24/7 access using the powerful Algolia search system, you can find relevant information quickly, easily and safely anytime from your laptop, tablet or smartphone, in class or at home.

Visit issuesonline.co.uk to find out more!

Chapter 1 The Facts

What is smoking?

Smoking is when you burn tobacco, most commonly in a cigarette, and breathe in the smoke. Tobacco contains nicotine, a highly addictive substance that can make it difficult for people to stop smoking once they have started. Although smoking rates have fallen in many countries, it remains one of the biggest causes of illness and death around the world.

People have used tobacco for hundreds of years, but today we know far more about the risks it poses to health. Cigarettes contain thousands of chemicals, many of which are harmful. When someone smokes, these chemicals enter the lungs and then travel around the body through the bloodstream.

Smoking is the leading cause of premature, preventable death globally. A premature death is one that happens earlier than expected, while a preventable death is one that could potentially be avoided. Tobacco kills up to half of its long-term users, which equates to around 7.5 million deaths every year worldwide. These deaths affect not only individuals but also families, communities, and healthcare systems.

One of the biggest dangers of smoking is its link to cancer. Smoking is the biggest cause of cancer in the world and can cause cancer in almost any part of the body. While many people associate smoking with lung cancer, it can also increase the risk of cancers of the mouth, throat, oesophagus, stomach, liver, pancreas, bladder, kidney, cervix, and more. In fact, being smoke free can help prevent 15 different types of cancer.

Smoking does not just increase the risk of cancer. It can damage nearly every organ in the body, including the heart, lungs, and blood vessels. Over time, smoking can make it harder to breathe, reduce physical fitness, and increase the risk of serious diseases such as heart disease and stroke.

Despite these risks, there is some positive news. Smoking rates in the United Kingdom have fallen significantly over recent years, particularly among younger adults. Since 2011, the largest fall in smoking prevalence has been among 18- to 34-year-olds, dropping from 25.7% in 2011 to 8.1% in 2024. Smoking prevalence among young people has also halved in the past ten years. This suggests that more young people are choosing not to smoke and are becoming more aware of the health risks associated with tobacco use.

However, smoking rates are not the same across all parts of society. In the UK, nearly one in five people in routine and manual occupations smoke (18.8%), compared with one in fifteen people in managerial and professional occupations (6.5%). This difference highlights how factors such as income, education, environment, and access to support can influence smoking rates.

Although fewer people are smoking than in the past, tobacco remains a major health challenge. Understanding what smoking is and the risks it carries can help people make informed decisions about their health. Choosing to stay smoke free is one of the most effective ways to protect your body and reduce the risk of serious illness in the future.

Tobacco

Tobacco is found in cigarettes which are smoked and shisha which is smoked through a waterpipe (hookah). Tobacco contains the addictive substance nicotine.

Tobacco, also called:

- Baccy
- Ciggies
- Fags
- Hookah
- Hubble bubble
- Roll-ups
- Rollies
- Shisha
- Smokes

How it looks, tastes and smells

What does it look like?

The leaves of the tobacco plant are picked, dried and then rubbed to produce a brown, flaky mixture.

It is sold as factory-made cigarettes or as rolling tobacco, which is used to make hand-rolled cigarettes (roll-ups). It is also sold as shisha, which is smoked using a waterpipe (hookah).

In the UK tobacco is sold in standard packs with no corporate branding and large picture health warnings.

Tobacco has a strong and distinctive taste and smell. As well as the tobacco smoke that is inhaled into a smoker's lungs, there is secondhand smoke which is made up of the smoke exhaled by the smoker and the 'sidestream' smoke from the tip of the cigarette. More than 80% of secondhand smoke is invisible and odourless.

How do people take it?

Cigarettes

Most people smoke tobacco in a cigarette. Cigarettes can be manufactured or hand-rolled using rolling tobacco.

Shisha

Shisha is flavoured tobacco that is smoked using a water pipe (hookah). The tobacco is burned in a bowl containing charcoal and the smoke is sucked through the water pipe, which cools the smoke down allowing it to be breathed in by the smoker.

Shisha is part of Middle Eastern and Indian culture, but it is also used in the UK among non-Middle Eastern and Indian groups.

Other types of tobacco include cigars, cigarillos and chewing tobacco.

How it feels

How does it make you feel?

How does it make you feel? Smoking gives you a hit of nicotine, which is the addictive substance in tobacco. Nicotine is a stimulant which raises your heart rate and blood pressure. First time smokers often feel sick and dizzy when they inhale nicotine for the first time.

Many smokers believe that smoking tobacco helps them to relax and handle stress. But smoking actually increases anxiety and tension. Smoking interferes with certain chemicals in the brain. When a smoker hasn't had a cigarette for a while, the craving for another one makes them feel irritable and anxious. These feelings can be temporarily relieved when they light up a cigarette which is why smokers associate their improved mood with smoking.

In fact, it's the effects of smoking itself that is more likely to have caused the anxiety in the first place. Cutting out smoking not only improves your mood but also reduces anxiety and stress.

The risks

Physical health risks

Tobacco smoke contains over 5,000 chemicals, many of which are poisonous, including more than 70 which can cause cancer. There is no 'safer' type of smoked tobacco – roll-up cigarettes, are just as harmful as manufactured cigarettes and smoking shisha through a waterpipe or hookah doesn't remove the toxic chemicals. These include:

- Tar – a mixture of dangerous chemicals
- Arsenic – used in wood preservatives/ rat poison
- Benzene – an industrial solvent, refined from crude oil
- Cadmium – used in batteries
- Ethanol – used in anti-freeze
- Formaldehyde – used in mortuaries to embalm dead bodies
- Polonium-210 – a highly radioactive element
- Chromium – used to manufacture dye, paints and alloys
- Acrolein – formerly used as a chemical weapon
- Hydrogen cyanide – used as an industrial pesticide
- Carbon Monoxide – contained in exhaust fumes
- Ammonia – used to make fertilisers and explosives.

Smoking damages nearly every organ of the body. It causes:

- Lung disease including emphysema and chronic bronchitis
- Heart and circulatory disease including heart attack, stroke and narrowing of the arteries

- At least 15 types of cancer including lung, mouth, throat, stomach, liver, kidney, bowel, bladder and cervix
- Reduced fertility in both men and women.

Smoking can cause bones to become weak and brittle, increasing the risk of osteoporosis in women. It also increases the risk of developing Type 2 diabetes, eye disease and dementia.

Smoking during pregnancy can harm the baby in the womb from conception onwards. Every cigarette smoked causes damage to both the mother-to-be and her baby. Smoking increases the risk of miscarriage, premature birth, stillbirth and sudden infant death syndrome. It makes it more likely that a woman will have life-threatening complications during pregnancy and labour, and that the baby will be too sick to go straight home after birth.

Smoking also harms other people around you. Being exposed to secondhand smoke can cause lung disease, heart disease and even cancer. Children are particularly at risk because they have less developed airways, lungs and immune systems.

Some people think shisha smoking is safer than cigarette smoking, but that isn't the case. People smoke shisha for much longer periods of time than they smoke a cigarette, and in one shisha session you can be exposed to very high levels of toxic chemicals. There is also the added risk of picking up diseases such as herpes, hepatitis C or tuberculosis from sharing waterpipes.

Mental health risks

Smoking increases anxiety and tension. Smokers are also more likely than non-smokers to develop depression over time.

Other effects from smoking:

Smoking tobacco has lots of immediate effects, such as making your breath, hair and clothes smell.

Smoking stops oxygen getting to the skin, making you more prone to spots and a dull complexion. Over time it can lead to premature aging, meaning more wrinkles and a so-called 'cat's bum' mouth.

The tar in tobacco smoke can lead to yellowed teeth and nails.

Addiction

Can you get addicted?

Yes. Tobacco contains nicotine, a highly addictive drug. Smoking any drug gets it to the brain very quickly. It takes just 8 to 10 seconds for the nicotine to reach the brain after tobacco smoke is inhaled. Smokers can get hooked very quickly and it can take years and a huge effort to kick the habit. Many people who smoke wish they hadn't started in the first place.

For advice on stopping smoking, visit the NHS Smoke free website: www.nhs.uk/smokefree or call the NHS Smokefree helpline on 0300 123 1044.

Worried about tobacco use?

If you are worried about your use, you can call FRANK on 0300 123 6600 for friendly, confidential advice.

The above information is reprinted with kind permission from FRANK.

www.talktofrank.com

Chemical Warning Cards

Instructions to student: Choose five chemicals found in tobacco smoke. For each one, write a warning card that explains where the chemical is also used and why it sounds dangerous. Finish by writing one sentence explaining why there is no 'safe' type of smoked tobacco.

What's in a cigarette?

Cigarette smoke contains over 5,000 chemicals. Many of these are poisonous and at least 70 cause cancer. Find out more about the chemicals in tobacco smoke, and how some of these lead to cancer.

Why are cigarettes harmful?

Cigarettes contain many dangerous chemicals. Some occur naturally in tobacco, and others are formed when processing tobacco into cigarettes. When a cigarette is burnt, it releases over 5,000 different chemicals in tobacco smoke. Many of these chemicals are harmful to people who smoke and also to people who breathe in secondhand smoke. We know that at least 70 of these chemicals cause cancer.

Roll-up tobacco cigarettes are not safer. They contain the same cancer-causing chemicals as manufactured cigarettes. Smoking using a filter, and smoking 'low-tar' or 'light' cigarettes also doesn't reduce the risk of disease from smoking. These are not safer or healthier options, and in the UK it is against the law to call tobacco products 'light', 'mild' or 'low-tar'.

Cigarettes are the most common type of tobacco used in the UK. But tobacco comes in many different forms. These include cigars, pipes, shisha and smokeless tobacco, such as paan or snus. All forms of tobacco are addictive and cause cancer, so there is no safe way to use tobacco.

What's in tobacco smoke?

Tar

Tar is a sticky-brown substance that collects in the lungs when tobacco smoke is breathed in. It can stain fingers and teeth a yellow-brown colour.

Tar contains cancer-causing chemicals. It also increases the risk of lung diseases, such as emphysema and chronic obstructive pulmonary disease (COPD).

Carbon monoxide

Tobacco smoke contains a poisonous gas called carbon monoxide. You can't smell it, see it or taste it.

Carbon monoxide stops the blood from carrying as much oxygen. This means organs of the body don't get the amount of oxygen they need, and the heart must work harder to supply the body with oxygen. This increases the risk of heart disease and stroke.

Nicotine

Nicotine is a very addictive chemical. Most people who smoke don't continue to do so out of choice – it's because they have a nicotine addiction.

Nicotine does not cause cancer. People have used nicotine replacement therapy (NRT) safely for many years to help them stop smoking. NRT helps people deal with cravings and nicotine withdrawal symptoms.

Over 5,000 different chemicals

Tobacco smoke is made up of thousands of chemicals. These include toxic metals, poisonous gases and chemicals that are known to cause cancer.

The chemicals in tobacco smoke mix when they are inhaled together and cause greater damage to the body. Some chemicals help other cancer-causing chemicals to damage the cells of the body.

What ingredients in cigarettes cause cancer?

At least 70 of the chemicals found in tobacco smoke cause cancer.

You may be surprised to learn where some of the cancer-causing chemicals in cigarettes are also used:

- 1,3-Butadiene is used in rubber manufacturing
- Arsenic is a poison
- Benzene is an industrial solvent, made from crude oil
- Beryllium is used in nuclear reactors
- Cadmium is used in batteries
- Chromium is used to manufacture dye, paint and car alloys
- Formaldehyde is used in science labs and mortuaries
- Polonium-21 is a highly radioactive element
- Polycyclic aromatic hydrocarbons are a group of dangerous chemicals found in oil and coal, including benzo(a)pyrene

How do chemicals in tobacco smoke lead to cancer?

Here are some of the ways that harmful chemicals in tobacco smoke damage the body:

Chemicals in tobacco smoke damage DNA

Our DNA controls how our cells grow and behave. DNA damage can cause cells to behave in ways they're not supposed to, which can lead to cancer.

Chemicals in tobacco smoke damage DNA. This includes the parts of DNA that protect our cells from becoming cancerous. There are also chemicals in tobacco smoke that stop our cells from repairing damaged DNA. This makes it even more likely that cancer will develop.

What's in a cigarette?

When a cigarette burns it releases a harmful mix of over 5000 chemicals - many can cause cancer.

Benzene
An industrial solvent, refined from crude oil

Chromium
Used to manufacture dye, paints and alloys

Polonium-210
A highly radioactive element

Cadmium
Used in batteries

Arsenic
A poison

Polycyclic aromatic hydrocarbons
A group of dangerous chemicals found in oil and coal

1,3-Butadiene
Used in rubber manufacturing

Formaldehyde
Used as a preservative in labs and mortuaries

Beryllium
Used in nuclear reactors

Source: Cancer Research UK

Chemicals in tobacco smoke harm the cleaning system in our airways

Chemicals in tobacco smoke damage the cilia in our airways. Cilia keep our airways clear from dirt and infections.

This means people who smoke are less able to clear toxic chemicals. The chemicals build up and cause damage. A cough is often developed as the lungs try to clear themselves.

Chemicals in tobacco smoke may affect our immune system and cause inflammation

Our immune system is designed to protect us. But some research suggests chemicals in tobacco smoke may affect how our immune system works. Chemicals in tobacco smoke have also been shown to cause inflammation, which can lead to DNA damage.

7 June 2023

What is nicotine – and how does Big Tobacco weaponise it?

Big Tobacco offers a wide menu of products, and positions each one a little differently. It implies that some are safer than others, but from cigarettes to hookahs to nicotine pouches to e-cigarettes and more, all of Big Tobacco's products have one major commonality: they all contain nicotine.

Nicotine is an addictive chemical found in tobacco plants. People inhale or ingest nicotine when they use tobacco products, like cigarettes, heated tobacco products, bidis, waterpipes, cigars, pipes or oral tobacco, or even products that don't contain tobacco, such as e-cigarettes* and nicotine pouches.

Whether or not a product contains tobacco, all products that contain nicotine are addictive. Nicotine is the reason why these products can be so difficult to quit, even for people who really want to. And the tobacco industry knows it.

The known (and unknown) harms of nicotine

While nicotine is not the key driver of some diseases caused by tobacco use, such as lung disease and a multitude of cancers, it has many side effects.

Nicotine is a stimulant and can temporarily make people feel more alert and improve their mood. It also has harmful side effects. After taking a puff of a cigarette, high doses of nicotine can reach the brain within seven seconds.

In the short term, nicotine can elevate your heart rate and increase your blood pressure. In the long term, it can lead to the narrowing of arteries or the hardening of arterial walls, which can increase the risk of a heart attack. And while nicotine isn't a carcinogen, some research suggests that it may play a role in cancer progression.

The delivery method of nicotine also comes with its own harms. E-cigarettes, which don't contain tobacco, can generate toxic substances, and their long-term effects on health are unknown.

Nicotine's negative side effects continue even after use. Nicotine withdrawal can lead to chest tightness, headaches, dizziness, gastrointestinal issues, psychological agitation, unease, fatigue and sadness or depression.

Even just handling tobacco leaves can subject people to the chemical's side effects. Tobacco growers are at risk of contracting green tobacco sickness, which causes headaches, nausea, vomiting, fatigue and other symptoms.

Nicotine is harmful to young people

Experts agree that nicotine is harmful to children and adolescents. Its toxic effects – even in doses as low as 1 to 4 milligrams – can include confusion, vomiting and loss of consciousness. In large doses, nicotine can be deadly to children.

As the popularity of e-cigarettes and nicotine pouches has increased, so have incidences of children ingesting these products. Reports of children ingesting the liquid nicotine found in e-cigarettes increased by almost 60% in the US between 2010 and 2015, with the majority of incidents involving children under the age of two. While ingestion of e-cigarette liquids dropped between 2015 and 2023, reports of children ingesting nicotine pouches increased by 763% between 2020 and 2023 – and these cases were more likely to have serious medical outcomes.

Nicotine is also harmful to adolescents – a key target market for the industry's products. The effects of nicotine on adolescent brain development can be long-lasting. Exposure to nicotine can affect the parts of the brain related to attention, learning, mood and impulse control. Nicotine can also increase stress levels and contribute negatively to teens' mental health.

> 'Nicotine is addictive. We are, then, in the business of selling nicotine, an addictive drug'
>
> – Executive at BAT subsidiary Brown and Williamson

The tobacco industry weaponised nicotine to sustain the tobacco epidemic

In 1994, the president of the US Tobacco Company told the US Congress, under oath, 'I don't believe that nicotine or our products are addictive.' Six other tobacco company CEOs testified alongside him. Not only was this false (industry documents show that tobacco companies had known for decades that nicotine was addictive), the industry had been intentionally manipulating its products to make them more addictive.

Tobacco and nicotine companies have been found to modify tobacco crops to deliver more nicotine. They have altered

their product designs to increase the amount of nicotine smokers consume. They've added ammonia to cigarettes to help nicotine reach the brain faster. They've underreported how much nicotine is in heated tobacco products, exposing users to up to eight times the amount of nicotine they thought they were getting. They've created e-cigarette cartridges that contain as much nicotine as 20 cigarettes and that, they claim, deliver nicotine 2.7 times faster than other e-cigarettes.

The industry benefits from a general lack of awareness around how much nicotine is in newer products such as e-cigarettes and nicotine pouches. In the US, the average nicotine concentration in e-cigarettes increased by 106% between 2013 and 2018. Disposable e-cigarettes, which are popular among young people around the world, may also have higher nicotine strengths.

Studies have also found that labelling on nicotine pouches is often misleading or insufficient, or sometimes missing altogether. Some pouches were found to have nicotine contents up to 50 mg per pouch (for reference, most people inhale 1 – 2 mg of nicotine per cigarette). Many users may not be aware that they might be consuming significantly more nicotine than if they used tobacco.

Now, the industry is leaning heavily on nicotine products to offset reductions in tobacco use in many parts of the world and protect its profits. All of the Big Four transnational tobacco companies have developed e-cigarettes and nicotine pouches, and many are finding ways to market them to young people.

The industry is creating a global youth nicotine epidemic

Big Tobacco may say its e-cigarettes and nicotine pouches are for adult smokers who want to move away from cigarettes, but evidence shows it targets these products at children and young people.

The industry designs nicotine products to appeal to young people. Companies add fruit and candy flavours to e-cigarettes and nicotine pouches. E-cigarette designs range from toy-like to sleek and high-tech, and are often marketed as lifestyle products. Tobacco companies market these products widely on social media. A Campaign for Tobacco-Free Kids report found that social media marketing promoting British American Tobacco (BAT)'s nicotine pouch reached over 10 million users under age 18, and promotion of its e-cigarette reached 4.3 million users under age 18.

As a result of the industry's efforts, e-cigarette and nicotine pouch use is growing among young people. There is also a risk of these products contributing to the tobacco epidemic: Research suggests that non-smokers who use e-cigarettes may be up to three times more likely to start smoking cigarettes than people who don't use e-cigarettes.

Policymakers can – and should – protect the next generation

In 1963, an executive at Brown and Williamson, a BAT subsidiary, said 'Nicotine is addictive. We are, then, in the business of selling nicotine, an addictive drug.' This still rings true today. And all people, especially the youngest generation, deserve to be protected from industry tactics that aim to entrap them in a lifetime of addiction.

Governments have the power to reduce, or even prevent, a youth nicotine epidemic in their country. The Conference of the Parties to the WHO Framework Convention on Tobacco Control (FCTC) has encouraged countries to ban or strictly regulate e-cigarettes. Age restrictions on nicotine products, regulating nicotine levels to reduce addiction, banning nicotine product advertising and increasing taxes on nicotine products are just some of the actions policymakers can take to protect the youngest generations.

**While not all commercial e-cigarettes contain nicotine, most do.*

6 October 2025

The above information is reprinted with kind permission from STOP and Vital Strategies.

www.exposetobacco.org

How long does nicotine stay in your system?

It typically takes 2 hours for half the nicotine to leave the body after ingesting it. After quitting smoking, a person may experience significant withdrawal symptoms from a few days to weeks or longer.

By Danielle Dresden

Nicotine is the addictive substance in tobacco, cigarettes, and vapes, also called e-cigarettes.

When people use tobacco products, some of the nicotine stays in their system after they quit smoking. Medical tests can detect nicotine in people's urine, blood, saliva, hair, and nails.

How long does nicotine stay in the body?

Nicotine has a half-life of around 2 hours . This means that 2 hours after ingesting it, the body will have removed around half of the nicotine.

This short half-life means that the immediate effects of nicotine go away quickly, so people soon feel like they need another dose.

When nicotine enters the body, it is broken down into more than 20 different substances, including cotinine, anabasine, and nornicotine. People eventually excrete these by-products in their urine.

Doctors can use nicotine tests to measure levels of nicotine and its by-products in a person's:

- urine
- blood
- saliva
- hair
- nails.

When a doctor is testing for tobacco use or exposure to nicotine, they will likely test for cotinine. This is because it stays in the body for longer.

It can take more than 2 weeks for a person's blood to reach the same cotinine levels as someone who does not use tobacco. It takes several more weeks for cotinine levels in urine to become very low.

Traces of nicotine may stay in the hair for longer, though people are rarely asked to do a hair test unless they are taking part in research.

The more someone smokes, and the higher the frequency of smoking, the longer nicotine takes to leave the body.

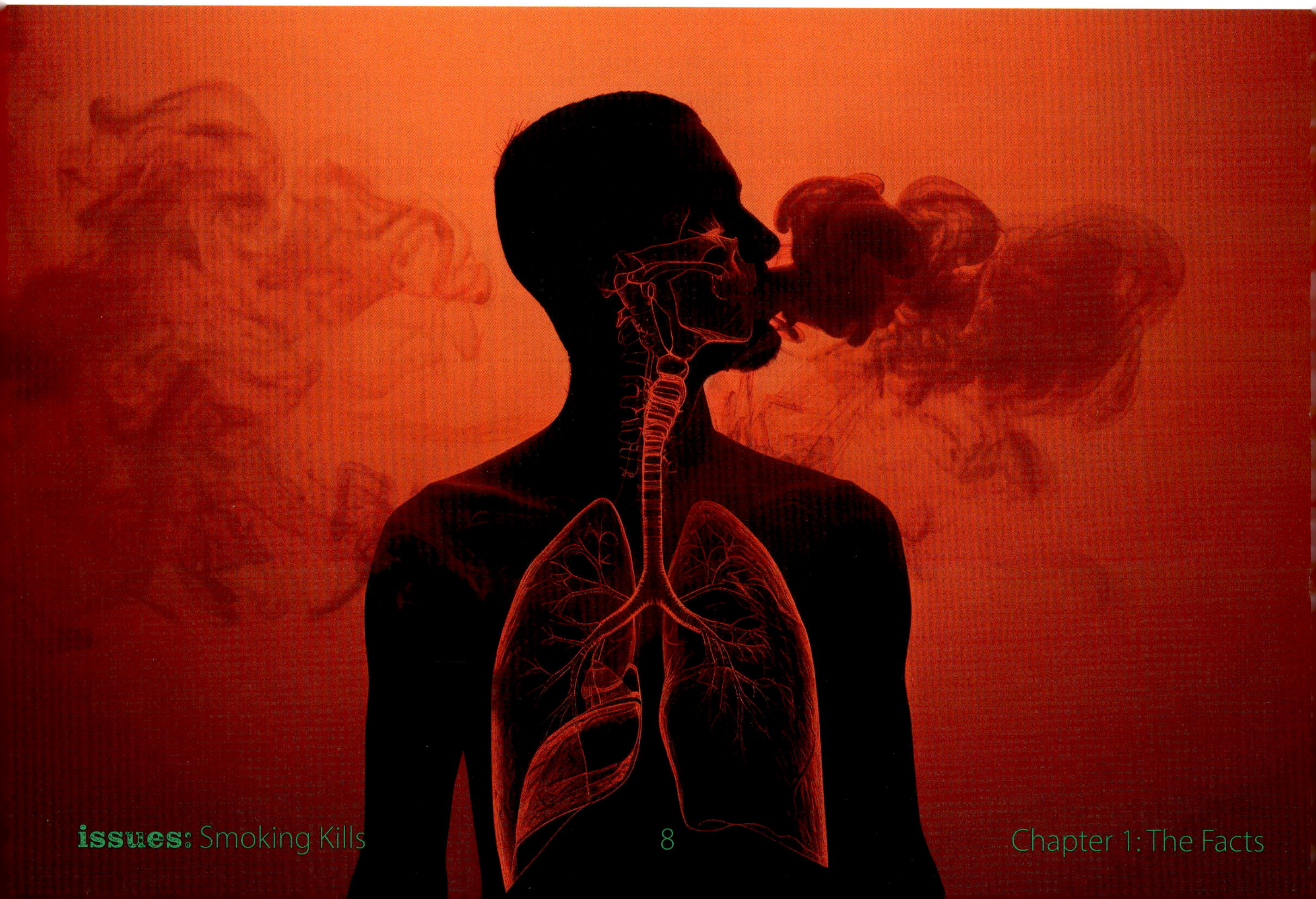

How long does nicotine withdrawal last?

The severity and timeline of physical withdrawal symptoms vary depending on how much an individual smokes.

Symptoms of nicotine withdrawal are at their worst during the first week after quitting, and they peak during the first 3 days. After this time, symptoms often lessen over time.

The physical and psychological effects of nicotine withdrawal include:

- anxiety
- stress
- irritability
- trouble sleeping
- depression
- restlessness
- difficulty focusing
- increased appetite.

Once the physical symptoms are gone and all nicotine has left the body, a person may still feel a psychological desire to smoke. Often, this is because they are used to the habit of smoking.

The desire for nicotine may be worse in triggering situations. Examples of these may include times of stress or when having drinks with friends. Over time, these triggers become much less powerful.

Smoking vs. vaping

Nicotine tests can detect nicotine in the body when people have used an electronic cigarette, also called a vape.

Vaping is a relatively recent invention, so little research has looked into its short- and long-term effects. Researchers do not yet know whether the body processes nicotine differently from cigarettes or vapes.

The content of nicotine in e-cigarettes is variable. For example, the Centers for Disease Control and Prevention (CDC) reports that some e-cigarettes marketed as containing no nicotine actually do contain nicotine.

Additionally, there is no consistency regarding the way nicotine strength is displayed on vape products. For example, different products may report nicotine levels in the following ways:

- a range from low to high
- percentage of nicotine per volume
- concentration
- amount of nicotine per amount of e-liquid.

The following factors may determine how much nicotine people ingest when using a vape or e-cigarette:

- amount of nicotine in the vaping solution
- efficiency with which vaping devices deliver nicotine
- differences in how people use vaping devices, including frequency and length of inhalation.

According to the Food and Drug Administration (FDA), there is **no safe tobacco** product.

Testing methods for nicotine

Testing people for nicotine is sometimes done for insurance or job-related reasons. Nicotine tests measure a person's exposure to nicotine and, if they have been exposed, by how much. These tests look for traces of nicotine and other related substances, such as cotinine.

Cotinine is a more reliable measure of tobacco use because it stays in the body for much longer. The half-life of nicotine is around 2 hours, while the half-life of cotinine is 15 to 20 hours.

Testing can use the following different parts of the body for tissue samples:

- urine
- saliva
- blood
- hair
- nails.

Can you clear nicotine from the body?

There is no sure way to flush the body of nicotine quickly, but people may try maintaining a healthy lifestyle so that their body works efficiently.

The following methods may help clear nicotine from the body:

- drinking plenty of water to flush waste products from the kidneys and liver
- exercising to get the blood moving, boost circulation, and release waste products through sweat
- eating a balanced diet rich in antioxidants to help the body repair itself.

Some commercial products and herbal remedies claim to speed up the body's ability to clear nicotine from the system, but regulators have not usually tested them scientifically.

Summary

The rate at which nicotine leaves the system is affected by:

- how much nicotine a person uses and how often
- how long a person has been using tobacco products
- the person's overall health and age.

It is not yet clear whether people who vape clear nicotine from their systems more rapidly than people who smoke traditional cigarettes.

4 October 2024

Why is smoking bad for you? The effects of smoking

Find out why smoking is bad for your lung health, as well as for the people around you. We also explain why it can be hard to stop smoking, and how breathing in any smoke is harmful.

What's in tobacco smoke?

Tobacco smoke contains over 5,000 chemicals, including nicotine. People who smoke do so because they are addicted to nicotine, but the harm comes from the tar, carbon monoxide, and other chemicals in the smoke.

Many of the chemicals can cause cancer. Others are poisonous. When you smoke, these chemicals damage your lungs and can pass into your blood and spread through your body. Smoking can affect every part of the body, from your skin to your brain.

Why should I stop smoking?

Stopping smoking is one of the best things you can do for your health. If you smoke and have a lung condition, one of the best treatments for your lungs is to stop smoking. You'll feel less short of breath and cough less.

If you stop smoking, you're likely to live longer, feel better, and have more money. You'll also protect people around you from having to breathe in your smoke. Passive smoking is harmful, especially for children and young people. Other reasons to stop smoking:

- If you have asthma and smoke, you will need higher doses of steroid preventer medicine to treat the inflammation in your airways.
- If you already have a lung condition, stopping smoking is the best step you can take for your health and quality of life. It will help you cope with your symptoms and stop your condition getting worse.
- Your friends and family will be healthier. People who breathe in secondhand smoke are at risk of the same diseases as people who smoke. Secondhand smoke is particularly dangerous to babies and children as their lungs are still developing.
- Smoking puts your lungs at risk – people who smoke are five times more likely to catch flu and twice as likely to get pneumonia.
- It's never too late to stop, no matter how long you have smoked for. Your lungs will work better, even if you stop when you're over 60. If you stop smoking when you're 30, you're likely to live 10 years longer.
- Stopping will protect your children's health in the long term. Children are more likely to take up smoking if their parents smoke.
- You'll save money. The average person who smokes can save around £38 a week by quitting smoking. Use the NHS inform calculator to work out how much money you could save if you quit smoking today.
- As well as being bad for your health, smoking is also bad for the environment. Smoking and the tobacco industry are linked with deforestation, corruption, child labour, and other human rights abuses.

What does smoking do to your lungs?

Smoking and breathing in secondhand smoke (passive smoking) causes many lung conditions, including:

- chronic obstructive pulmonary disease (COPD)
- obstructive sleep apnoea (OSA)
- pneumonia
- lung cancer.

The NHS says 35% of all deaths for respiratory conditions are linked to smoking. If you smoke and have a lung condition, the most effective treatment is to stop smoking. Read more about how you can quit.

People who smoke are at higher risk of getting chest infections, including flu, pneumonia, and COVID-19 . If you smoke and get an infection, you're more likely to have severe symptoms.

Smoking doesn't just affect your lungs. It also causes:

- heart attacks
- strokes
- other cancers
- skin aging
- erectile dysfunction
- infertility.

On average, people who smoke live 10 years less than non-smokers. Smoking tobacco is the leading cause of preventable deaths in the UK.

Why can quitting smoking be hard?

The tobacco industry has designed cigarettes to be as addictive as possible. Their advertising is also marketed at young people.

The nicotine in tobacco gets into your brain and creates a need to continue to smoke. When you stop smoking, the falling level of nicotine in your brain creates the urge to smoke. Controlling these urges is the best way to quit.

Smoking is often part of your daily routine and becomes a habit. Your local stop smoking service can support you to manage this side of smoking, as well as helping with physical cravings.

Are all types of smoking bad?

There's no safe way to smoke tobacco. Tobacco comes in different forms, which are all harmful and addictive:

- Low tar, light or menthol cigarettes are not safer than other cigarettes. Many of these types of cigarettes are banned in the UK, but are still available abroad. You get similar amounts of tar and other chemicals from these cigarettes.
- Roll-ups are just as dangerous as factory-made cigarettes. Filters do not make smoking any safer and are a type of plastic pollution
- Cigars or pipes are not a safe alternative to cigarettes. Cigar smoke contains more chemicals than other cigarettes.
- Shisha smoking often contains tobacco, but it's the burnt charcoal that increases the harm. The smoke goes through water but still contains the same dangerous chemicals and is just as harmful as other cigarette smoke.

Cannabis smoking

Breathing in any type of smoke is harmful. This includes cannabis, also known as marijuana, weed, pot, dope, or grass. Cannabis smoking is linked with getting COPD and can make asthma symptoms worse.

You can become addicted to cannabis, and just like tobacco, cannabis smoke has cancer-causing chemicals. If you mix cannabis with tobacco and smoke it, you're at risk of becoming addicted to nicotine too.

Cannabis is also linked with an increased risk of getting schizophrenia.

Shisha

Shisha, also called hookah, narghile, waterpipe, or hubble bubble, is a form of smoking tobacco. It's addictive and harmful for your health. Smoking shisha can at least double your risk of getting lung cancer and could also increase your risk of other cancer types, such as mouth or stomach cancers.

Smoking shisha is a risk for people with asthma and can increase the chance of asthma attacks.

Smokeless tobacco

Smokeless tobacco is tobacco that isn't burned. It's often chewed, sucked, or breathed in. There are different types of smokeless tobacco. The products are often known by their south Asian names, such as betel quid, paan, or gutkha.

Smokeless tobacco is addictive and harmful for your health. It's linked with mouth cancer, cardiovascular disease, and problems in pregnancy. As well as tobacco, it can also include other harmful ingredients such as slaked lime, betel nut or areca nut, which are known to cause cancer too.

Examples of smokeless tobacco are:

- tobacco with or without flavourings, such as mishri India powdered tobacco and qimam, also known as kimam
- tobacco with slaked lime or lime paste and areca nut, such as paan, gutkha, zarda, mawa, manipuri and betel quid with tobacco
- tobacco with other ingredients added, such as kahini, gul, and naswar, also called niswar or nass.

31 March 2024

www.asthmaandlung.org.uk

Understanding the true impact of smoking

You probably know smoking is harmful, but you might not realise how much it affects your body and every part of your life.

From your health to your mood and your loved ones, smoking can have a bigger impact than you think.

But the good news is that once you quit, you'll notice positive changes almost straight away, proving that it's never too late to quit!

How smoking impacts your mind

Many people think that smoking helps calm their nerves and reduces anxiety. It might feel like a cigarette eases stress or tension, but the truth is it can make things feel worse.

Smoking gives a quick hit of nicotine, which feels relaxing at first, but that feeling fades fast.

When it wears off, you can feel even more anxious, stressed or down. This can lead to smoking more often, but, instead of fixing the problem, it can create a cycle where anxiety and depression get worse, not better.

The good news

When you quit smoking, the natural chemicals in your brain, like dopamine, start to balance out, which helps lift your mood. Over time, you will feel happier, less anxious, and more in control of your life.

How smoking impacts your body

Most people know smoking causes heart disease and a wide range of cancers, but may not realise just how far-reaching its damage can be.

Smoking can cause:

Hearing and vision loss

Studies show that smoking increases the risk of hearing loss and eye problems like cataracts, glaucoma, dry eyes, and vision damage as you age.

Dementia

The UK Alzheimer's Society says smoking increases the risk of dementia. It damages blood vessels, which is linked to Alzheimer's disease and vascular dementia. Chemicals in smoke also harm cells and cause inflammation, making the risk even higher.

Damage to your joints

Smoking increases inflammation in the body, which can worsen joint pain and damage. It also increases the risk of rheumatoid arthritis, back pain, shoulder tears and osteoporosis.

Digestive issues

Studies show that smoking can harm your digestive system, causing issues like heartburn, ulcers, liver problems, and a higher risk of Crohn's disease, pancreatitis, and gallstones.

High blood pressure

Blood Pressure UK warns that smoking damages blood vessels, narrows arteries, and puts extra strain on your heart by raising your blood pressure.

High blood pressure often has no symptoms, so getting checked is the only way to know.

If you are 40 or over in England, you can get a free blood pressure check at your pharmacy today.

The good news

The good news is your body will start to heal almost immediately after you quit. Within just 20 minutes, your pulse rate will return to normal.

After 8 hours, harmful chemicals like carbon monoxide in your blood will have halved, making room for more oxygen to flow through your body.

And after 10 years, your risk of dying from lung cancer is half that of someone who still smokes.

How smoking impacts your finances

If you need extra motivation to quit smoking, think about how much of your monthly income is spent on smoking.

Imagine you spend £14 on a pack of cigarettes. Here's what smoking half a pack a day adds up to over time:

- 1 month would cost around £213
- 6 months would cost around £1,277
- 1 year would cost around £2,555
- 5 years would cost around £12,775
- 10 years would cost around £25,550

This does not even account for the extra costs of smoking-related health problems!

The good news

Quitting smoking gives you a lot more disposable income every month. Imagine the possibilities! You could:

- ✔ pay off a small debt or catch up on bills
- ✔ stock up on groceries or household essentials
- ✔ treat your family to a day out or special meal
- ✔ save for Christmas or birthday presents
- ✔ put it towards something you need, like a washing machine or phone repair

What would you do with this extra money in your pocket?

How smoking impacts your looks

Smoking not only harms your health but also affects your appearance in ways you might not expect.

Did you know that smoking:

- makes your skin age faster, causing wrinkles and sagging
- stains your teeth, turning them yellow over time
- reduces oxygen to your skin, leaving it looking tired and dull
- can cause your hair to thin and fall out
- can turn your fingers and nails yellow
- weakens your hair and nails, making them break easily
- make skin conditions like acne or psoriasis much worse

The good news

Quitting smoking helps your skin heal and look healthier. In just a few days, blood flow improves, giving your skin much more oxygen and nutrients.

Wrinkles may look less noticeable, your complexion can brighten, and you'll stop causing further damage. It's one more reason to stay strong on your journey!

How smoking impacts your loved ones

When you smoke, most of the smoke goes into the air around you, where others can breathe it in.

This secondhand smoke can harm your family and friends, increasing their risk of lung cancer, heart disease and breathing problems.

Secondhand smoke is especially harmful to children and pregnant women.

The good news

Quitting smoking not only protects your health but also creates a safer environment for your loved ones.

Once you stop, secondhand smoke is no longer a risk to your family, giving them cleaner air to breathe and a healthier future.

You are stronger than your habit!

Smoking harms your health, costs money, and hurts those around you. Quitting can change all of that.

Every cigarette you refuse is a step toward better health, more energy, and more money in your pocket.

You can protect your friends and family and give yourself a better future. It is never too late to quit, and every small effort makes a difference.

Keep going, and you will start to feel the benefits of quitting!

www.nhs.uk

Mood Myth Buster

Many people believe smoking helps with stress. Create a short 'myth versus fact' explanation that shows why this is misleading. Include the quick nicotine hit, the return of anxiety or low mood, and how quitting can help brain chemicals become more balanced over time.

The Cost of Smoking

Use the figures in the article to create a simple money plan. Imagine someone quits after spending £14 on cigarettes every few days. Choose three things they could do with the money saved over one year, then explain which option would have the biggest positive impact.

Children whose fathers smoked during puberty may age faster

Signs of premature biological ageing found in offspring of males addicted to tobacco as a young teenager.

Children whose fathers smoked during puberty age faster, a study has suggested.

Experts said smoking among boys aged 15 and younger could damage developing sperm cells, which could affect their future children.

The study, presented to the European Respiratory Society Congress in Amsterdam, found signs of faster biological ageing, compared with actual age, among people whose fathers began smoking in this age bracket.

Researchers examined the markers of ageing in a person's DNA, sometimes referred to as an epigenetic clock.

They looked for these epigenetic changes in blood samples of 892 people from various European countries and Australia, ranging in age from 7 to 50.

The subjects were asked whether they or their parents had ever smoked and at what age.

People whose fathers began smoking during puberty were around nine months to a year older than their chronological age on average.

If the person had smoked themselves, the differences were 'more pronounced', the authors reported.

Among those whose fathers began smoking later in life, researchers found only a small increase in biological age.

They found no clear pattern in biological ageing in people whose mothers smoked before pregnancy.

Presenting the study, Dr Juan Pablo Lopez-Cervantes, from the University of Bergen, Norway, said: 'Our research group has previously shown that smoking during puberty may harm not only the person who smokes, but also their future children.

'In this new study, we wanted to explore whether parental smoking in puberty may also influence the biological ageing of their future children.

The dangers of smoking as a child

It doubles the risk of premature death and significantly increases respiratory problems, cancer and other serious health conditions, say experts.

Early smoking can also impact lung growth, cause skin and teeth issues, and lead to irritability and difficulty concentrating due to nicotine addiction.

Children who smoke are more prone to coughs, wheezing and shortness of breath, and can hinder lung growth as well as lead to discoloured teeth and fingers and premature skin aging.

They are more likely to start smoking if parents, siblings or friends smoke and growing up in an environment where smoking is normalised, such as a home with smokers, increases the risk.

Tips to stop smoking

Seek help to stop smoking and your chances of quitting will increase

- Stop-smoking services are available through the NHS. Contact your GP for guidance.
- Book an appointment with your GP to enquire about varenicline or other daily stop-smoking pills.
- Know when you're tempted to smoke (e.g., on social occasions) and have a strategy, whether it's an e-cigarette, gum or a simple 'rule' that you can invoke, such as 'not a puff'.
- Vapes and e-cigarettes aren't perfect but they're 'far, far less harmful' than smoking, the experts say. If you're new to vaping, find one that uses nicotine salts, as the nicotine is coated like it is in cigarettes (albeit in cigarettes it's coated in toxic chemicals), making it less harsh on your throat.

'Accelerated biological ageing is important as it has been linked to a higher risk of diseases such as cancer, arthritis and dementia in previous research.'

He added: 'Our results suggest that boys who smoke during puberty may be unknowingly creating harm for the children they go on to have.

'This research does not fully explain why smoking in puberty is linked to faster ageing, but we think that when fathers start smoking during puberty, it may alter the epigenetic material of their sperm cells, and that these changes may be passed on to the next generation.

'Although this research is still in its early days, we believe our findings are important for young boys who smoke or consume other types of nicotine products.

'Stronger efforts to prevent tobacco use in adolescence should be a priority for policy-makers.'

Sarah Sleet, chief executive of Asthma and Lung UK, said: 'This research highlights why we must do everything we can to keep children away from smoking and help them stop if they have started.

'Adequate funding for smoking cessation services is vital. You are three times more likely to quit smoking successfully if you have a combination of counselling support and treatment to help relieve cravings and break tobacco dependence.'

Dr Stamatoula Tsikrika, chairman of the European Respiratory Society's expert group on tobacco, smoking control and health education, said: 'We all know that smoking causes diseases. What we're starting to learn is that the damage caused by smoking can persist across generations, passing the damage on to children.

'Although rates of smoking in teenagers seem to be declining, rates of vaping are generally increasing, and we don't yet know the long-term impact of vaping on children and teenagers. This research is another reminder that we need to protect children and teenagers from nicotine addiction, smoking and vaping.'

29 September 2025

www.telegraph.co.uk

Questions

1. What did the study suggest could happen to children whose fathers smoked during puberty?
2. Why do researchers think smoking during puberty may affect future children?
3. What is an epigenetic clock, and how was it used in the study?
4. How did the biological age of people whose fathers smoked during puberty compare with their actual age?
5. Why did experts say preventing smoking and nicotine use among teenagers should be a priority?

Puberty and Future Health

Create a simple cause-and-effect chain showing how boys smoking during puberty could affect their future children. Include smoking, possible changes to sperm cells, epigenetic changes, faster biological ageing and possible health risks later in life.

Study Snapshot

Write five short bullet points about the study. Include who was studied, what researchers looked at, what they found, and why it matters.

Smokers lose up to 22 minutes of life with a single cigarette, new predictions by experts warn

'The sooner smokers get off this escalator of death, the longer and healthier they can expect their lives to be,' new study says.

By Maya Oppenheim, Women's Correspondent

Women lose 22 minutes of their life with each cigarette they smoke while one shortens a man's life by 17 minutes, experts have estimated.

New predictions by researchers are higher than previous estimates which suggested that each cigarette shortens a smoker's life by 11 minutes.

The latest findings, which claim that each cigarette leads to a 20-minute loss of life on average across both genders, are based on more up-to-date figures from long-term studies tracking the health of the population.

Researchers from University College London said that the harm caused by smoking is 'cumulative' and the sooner a person stops smoking, and the more cigarettes they avoid smoking, the longer they live.

The new research, commissioned by the Department for Health and Social Care, suggests that if a 10-cigarettes-a-day smoker quits on 1 January, then by 8 January they could 'prevent loss of a full day of life'.

By 20 February, their lives could be extended by a whole week. And if their quitting is successful until 5 August, they will likely live for a whole month longer than if they had continued to smoke.

The authors said: 'Studies suggest that smokers typically lose about the same number of healthy years as they do total years of life.

'Thus smoking primarily eats into the relatively healthy middle years rather than shortening the period at the end of life, which is often marked by chronic illness or disability.

'So a 60-year-old smoker will typically have the health profile of a 70-year-old non-smoker.'

The analysis, which will be published in the Journal of Addiction, states the average of 20 minutes of life expectancy lost for each cigarette 'is time that would likely be spent in relatively good health'.

It adds: 'Stopping smoking at every age is beneficial but the sooner smokers get off this escalator of death, the longer and healthier they can expect their lives to be.'

Dr Sarah Jackson, principal research fellow from the UCL Alcohol and Tobacco Research Group, said: 'It is vital that people understand just how harmful smoking is and how much quitting can improve their health and life expectancy.'

'Every cigarette smoked costs precious minutes of life, and the cumulative impact is devastating, not only for individuals but also for our healthcare system and economy'

– Professor Sanjay Agrawal

She added: 'The sooner a person stops smoking, the longer they live. Quitting at any age substantially improves health and the benefits start almost immediately.

'It's never too late to make a positive change for your health and there are a range of effective products and treatments that can help smokers quit for good.'

Health officials say smokers can find advice, support and resources with the NHS Quit Smoking app, as well as the online Personal Quit Plan.

Public health minister Andrew Gwynne said: 'Smoking is an expensive and deadly habit and these findings reveal the shocking reality of this addiction, highlighting how important it is to quit.

'The new year offers a perfect chance for smokers to make a new resolution and take that step.'

Professor Sanjay Agrawal, special adviser on tobacco at the Royal College of Physicians, added: 'Every cigarette smoked costs precious minutes of life, and the cumulative impact is devastating, not only for individuals but also for our healthcare system and economy.

'This research is a powerful reminder of the urgent need to address cigarette smoking as the leading preventable cause of death and disease in the UK.'

2 January 2025

What are the current smoking rules?

Smokers are being encouraged to use a national awareness day to quit cigarettes for good.

Wednesday, 12 March marks No Smoking Day 2025, an annual campaign aimed at increasing awareness of resources available to support quitting smoking.

The NHS states that they hope the day could be the driving factor to helping people, offering services such as Nicotine Replacement Therapy (NRT) through the use of gum and patches.

But if you are still a smoker, what are the rules for lighting up?

What are the current UK smoking rules?

The current legal age for buying cigarettes and other tobacco products across the UK is 18 years old, the same as for alcohol.

This is also the age that teenagers become legal adults, enabling them to vote and access various other rights.

Smoking has been prohibited by law in virtually all enclosed and substantially enclosed workplaces and public places throughout the United Kingdom since July 2007. Smoke-free legislation in England forms part of the Health Act 2006 and The Children and Families Act 2014.

How have smoking rules changed in the past?

The legal age to buy cigarettes was raised from 16 in 2007 by the last Labour government, the first change to the age since 1908.

In July 2007, it also became illegal throughout the UK to smoke in any pub, restaurant, nightclub, and most workplaces and work vehicles.

What else is the Government trying to do to stop smokers?

In July, during the King's speech at the opening of Parliament, Labour laid out a pledge to bring back the proposal that would gradually raise the legal age of cigarette purchase.

If the proposed smoking ban goes ahead, a 14-year-old today will not be able to lawfully purchase cigarettes under the planned smoking ban. Labour also outlined intentions to restrict the marketing and sales of vapes. As well as creating a smoke-free generation, the government's Tobacco and Vapes Bill will extend the current indoor smoking ban to some outdoor settings, including children's playgrounds, outside schools and hospitals.

It was first thought smoking could also be banned in pub gardens, but after criticism, this did not appear in the Bill's laid-out plans, which are currently making their way through Parliament.

There is still little detail on how the rules would be policed. Health Secretary Wes Streeting said there would be a 'genuine consultation' on the measures following the passage of the Bill through Parliament.

Downing Street previously said it believes that recent government proposals of raising the legal smoking age will mean up to 1.7 million fewer people smoking by 2075, but it's not the only measure in place to reduce the number of smokers in the UK.

Tobacco products were also taxed at a higher rate since the Autumn Budget of 2021, when the Government announced that hand-rolling tobacco duty would increase in 2022 and 2023 by an additional four percentage points.

12 March 2025

What is the tobacco industry?

It's a simple question, but there's more to the answer than you might think. The tobacco industry isn't just made up of major tobacco companies and it doesn't just produce cigarettes. And, notably, selling its products isn't the industry's only business goal.

Take a closer look to get the facts about what the tobacco industry is and what it does – including the parts it may not want the public to focus on.

How big is the tobacco industry?

The world's largest transnational tobacco companies are known as the Big 4, and include Philip Morris International (PMI), British American Tobacco (BAT), Japan Tobacco International (JTI) and Imperial Brands. The China National Tobacco Corporation is the world's largest producer of cigarettes, but is a state-owned entity and mostly serves its own domestic market. Together, these companies sell trillions of cigarettes around the world every year, ensuring the tobacco epidemic continues and securing their future profits at the expense of public health.

The tobacco industry is present in nearly every country. In addition to smaller tobacco companies operating in specific countries or regions, the Big 4 run local subsidiaries around the world. For example, British American Tobacco South Africa is a local subsidiary of BAT, which is headquartered in the UK

While these major tobacco companies are the most visible players in the industry, other people and companies contribute to the industry's business, too, including tobacco farmers and processors, logistics companies and more. A deeper look at the tobacco industry's supply chain reveals the intricate and vast web of companies that play a role in producing and selling tobacco all over the world.

Then there are tobacco industry allies. These companies and organisations don't make or sell tobacco products, but they work with the industry to help further its business. Some allies openly promote the interests of the industry, such as tobacco trade groups, while others help advance the industry's agenda more discreetly. Some organisations' names even make it sound like they're working against the industry, such as the Global Action to End Smoking (formerly FSFW) or the Eliminating Child Labour in Tobacco-Growing Foundation. A look below the surface quickly shows that both of these groups are funded, wholly and in part, respectively, by the tobacco industry and often end up promoting industry-aligned agendas and narratives. Taking allies' messaging at face value without looking beneath the surface makes it easy to mistake these organisations as independent and miss their connections to the industry.

7 million deaths every year are caused by tobacco use

What products does the tobacco industry sell?

The tobacco industry is most recognised for selling cigarettes. Even though tobacco use is declining in many parts of the world, over 4.5 trillion cigarettes are projected to be consumed in 2025. Some major tobacco companies claim they want to move away from cigarettes, but analysis of their shareholder meetings and other business activities suggest cigarettes are still their cornerstone product and will remain so if no policy interventions are made.

The industry makes money off of other addictive tobacco products, as well. Bidis are small hand-rolled cigarettes that deliver more nicotine, tar and carbon monoxide than other cigarettes. They're produced primarily in India by a workforce of which up to 25% are children. Snus is another addictive tobacco product, sold as loose tobacco or in pouches that are placed between the gum and upper lip. Use of snus is associated with higher risk of pancreatic cancer.

Heated tobacco products (HTPs) are the industry's newest tobacco product. They're electronic devices that purport to heat tobacco versus burning it. Each of the Big 4 sells an HTP, but PMI's product, IQOS, has the biggest share of the HTP market. HTPs are marketed as so-called 'reduced-risk products,' even though the long-term health effects of these addictive tobacco products are still unknown.

The tobacco industry also sells addictive nicotine products that don't contain tobacco, including e-cigarettes, like BAT's Vuse, as well as nicotine pouches. Recent research has unearthed concerning evidence that the industry is attempting to addict young people to these newer nicotine and tobacco products by portraying them as high-tech, sophisticated lifestyle products.

What else is the industry involved in?

The tobacco industry isn't just in the business of making, marketing and selling tobacco products. It also spends considerable time and money funding and promoting misleading science, lobbying and performing so-called corporate social responsibility activities. All of these tactics and more are part of the industry's larger strategy to influence policies to favour its own commercial interests over public health.

The industry has also been accused of involvement in the illicit tobacco trade. While it may seem counterintuitive to facilitate the illegal sale of its own products, the illicit trade may actually benefit the tobacco industry – it can be a way to enter new markets, hook new users and open the door for interactions with government officials, which defies the World Health Organization Framework Convention on Tobacco Control (WHO FCTC).

Concerningly, the tobacco industry has tried to move into the pharmaceutical space. A notable example is PMI's failed acquisition of Vectura, a medical inhaler company whose products may be used to treat diseases associated with tobacco use. These types of acquisitions are likely the industry's attempt to diversify how it earns money and gain reputational benefits from being perceived as part of the health sector, despite its products causing eight million deaths every year.

How can we stop the tobacco industry?

The tobacco industry can't be trusted to self-regulate or provide safe, reliable solutions to the tobacco epidemic it created. History has shown that its actions ultimately serve to strengthen its own financial standing, which gives it the power to exploit low- and middle-income countries and influence policy around the world.

Governments must stand up to the industry. Many currently do, protecting their populations with higher tobacco taxes, advertising bans, age-related sales restrictions, mandated smoke-free spaces, graphic pack warnings and more. But the latest Global Tobacco Industry Interference Index shows that more must be done. Countries that are Parties to the WHO FCTC must fully implement and honour their commitments to the global health treaty.

Tobacco control measures must also be supported and implemented around the world. These proven measures can reduce tobacco use which leads to improved public health and more productive societies.

Ultimately, the tobacco industry's duplicitous behaviour must be exposed. Thanks to researchers' analyses, advocates' tireless work and whistleblowers who report potentially unlawful or unethical behaviour, the world's view of the industry's inner workings is clearer than ever.

12 February 2026

The above information is reprinted with kind permission from STOP and Vital Strategies

www.exposetobacco.org

Mapped: The UK regions where smoking is most common after stark new figures released

Smokers are getting through billions of cigarettes a year on average, new data shows.

By Albert Toth

Which region smokes the most cigarettes?

A study from Cancer Research UK and University College London (UCL) has revealed that Brits smoke 28.6 billion cigarettes a year

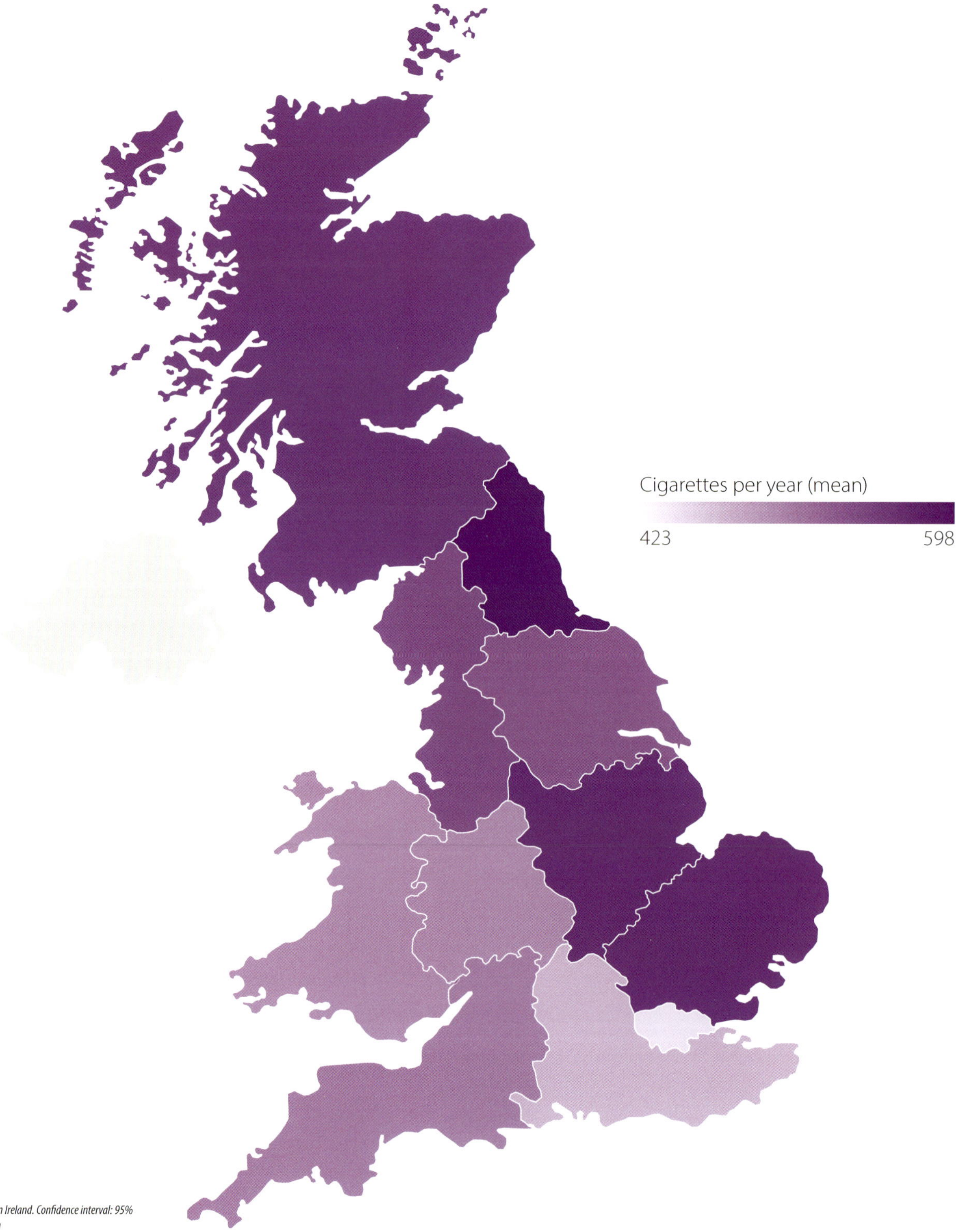

Note: Data not available for Northern Ireland. Confidence interval: 95%
Source: Nicotine & Tobacco Research

The number of cigarettes smoked in Britain every year has been revealed in a shocking new study from Cancer Research UK and University College London (UCL).

Smokers are getting through an estimated 28.6 billion cigarettes each year on average, equating to 78 million every day.

The study draws on data from the Smoking Toolkit Study between 2022 and 2024. It estimates that adults who smoke consume an average of 10.4 cigarettes daily, with 5.5% of smokers exceeding 20 cigarettes a day

The figures are also broken down by region, showing which areas in the UK have the highest proportion of smokers, and which region has the highest average number of cigarettes smoked.

The data shows that it is the South West that has the highest proportion of smokers at 15% of the adult population. Meanwhile, Scotland and Yorkshire are joint-lowest at 13.3%. Amongst all adults, the average is 13.9%.

However, smokers in southern regions smoke proportionally less cigarettes a year than those in the north and Scotland. Smokers in the North East average 598 cigarettes a year – the highest of any region – while London is the lowest at 423.

The analysis finds that this points to significant inequalities in cigarette consumption, with individuals from more deprived backgrounds smoking an average of 11 cigarettes daily, compared to 9.4 per day among those in wealthier areas.

In light of the figures, charities are calling on the government to speed up its upcoming Tobacco and Vapes Bill which is currently passing through Parliament. The legislation aims to create a 'smoke-free generation' by preventing the sale of tobacco products to anyone born on or after 1st January, 2009, effectively raising the legal smoking age each year.

Cancer Research UK's executive director of policy, Dr Ian Walker, said: 'While great strides have been made to bring down smoking rates, we can't afford to be complacent. Every week, around 550 million cigarettes are still smoked in Britain – that's enough to fill an Olympic sized swimming pool. It's vital that everyone, wherever they live, can access the support they need to quit smoking for good.

'The Tobacco and Vapes Bill is a historic opportunity to help stub out the harms of smoking, but it's frustrating that the legislation isn't progressing through Parliament as quickly as it should be.

'Tobacco is a toxic product that should have no place in our future, and I urge all parliamentarians to back a smoke-free UK and prioritise this Bill when it returns to the House of Lords. This world-leading legislation has strong political and public support that can't be ignored.'

18 July 2025

Smoking prevalence

While global smoking prevalence decreased from 22.7% in 2007 to 17% in 2021, in many countries there was either no change or prevalence increased. In several regions, despite a reduction in per capita consumption, total consumption has increased significantly due to a much faster increase in the number of smokers. In some countries, a combination of rapid economic growth and aggressive industry marketing generates a higher risk of future significant increases in smoking.

Although global smoking prevalence has declined (from 22.7% in 2007 to 17% in 2021), the total number of smokers remains high due to population growth. Globally, at least 940 million males and 193 million females ages 15 or older were current smokers in 2019. More than 75% of male daily smokers live in a country with a medium or high human development index (HDI), whereas more than 53% of female daily smokers live in very high-HDI countries.

Male smoking prevalence in most medium-to-very high-HDI countries substantially increased in the 20th century, though this generally happened earlier (the first half of the century) in very high-HDI countries. Almost all very high-HDI countries saw a significant decrease in male smoking after the 1950s. Many medium- or high-HDI countries also have seen a decline in prevalence from the beginning of the 21st century, but for the most part the decline was

Distribution of smokers

Male and female adult smokers (age 15+ years), 2019, by country HDI

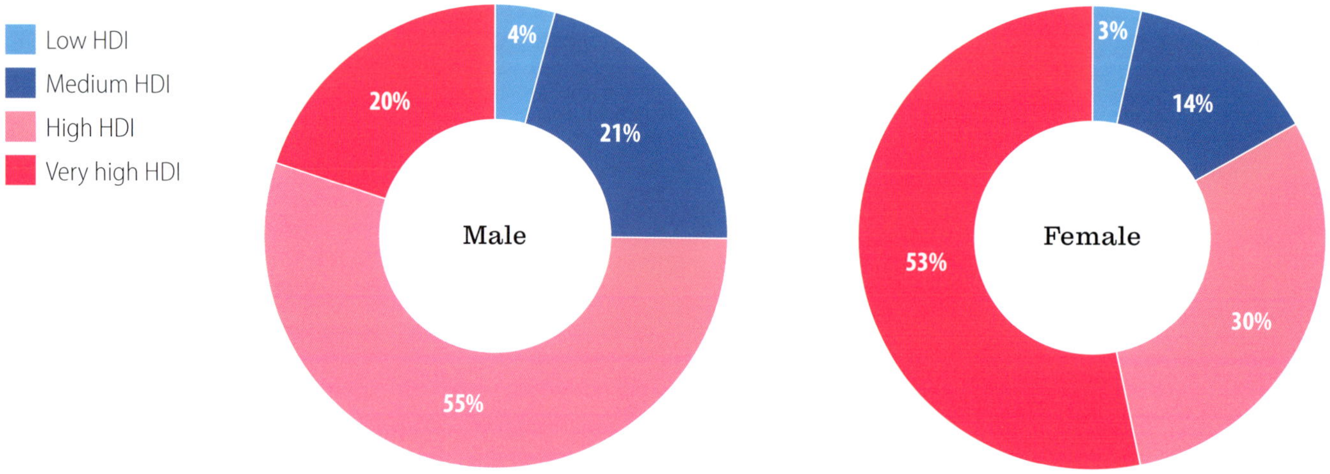

Three-quarters of current male daily smokers live in medium- or high-HDI countries, whereas more than half of female daily smokers live in very high-HDI countries.

Source: GBD, 2019

Changes in consumption

Percentage change in per capita cigarette consumption and number of smokers, 1990–2019, by WHO region

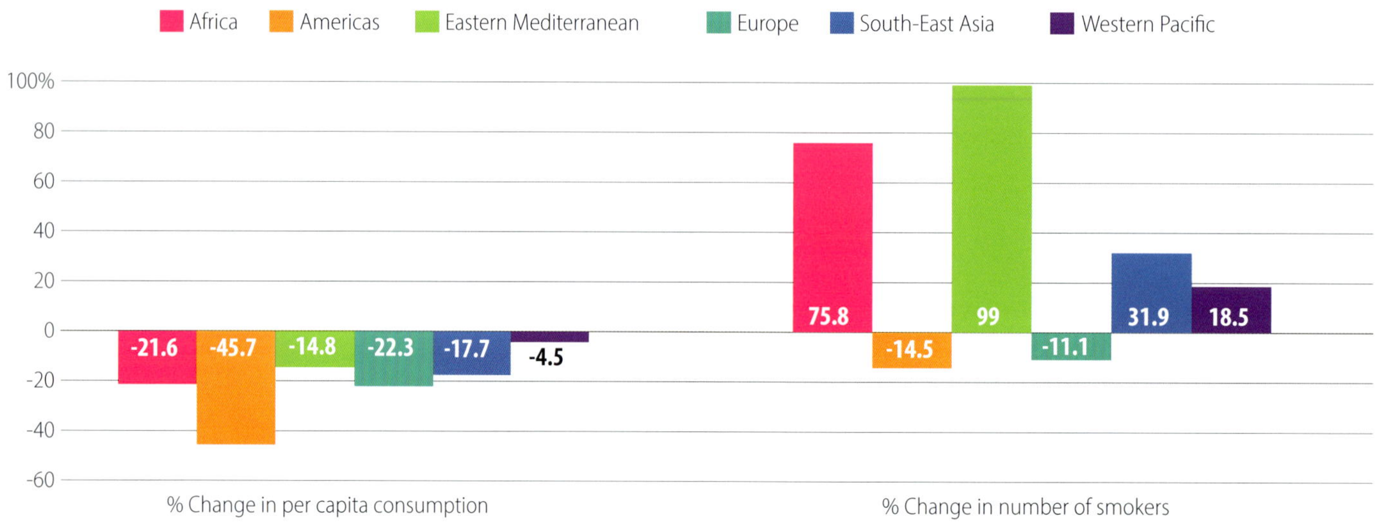

While consumption per capita has declined in all regions, the number of smokers has significantly increased in four out of six regions.

Source: GBD, 2019

Current smoking prevalence

Percentage of daily smokers: age 15+, 2021 or latest data available

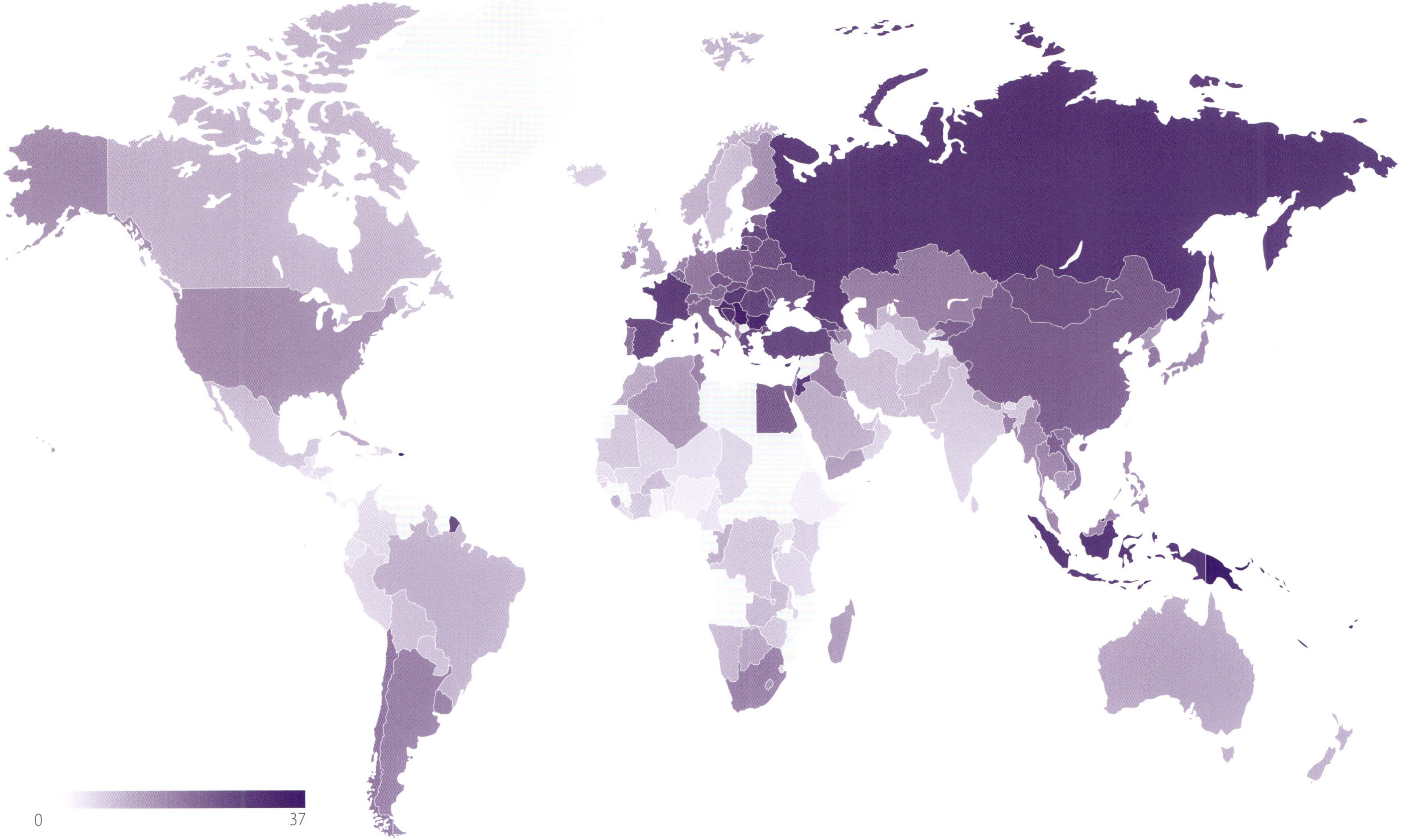

Overall smoking prevalence is declining but there are still more than one billion smokers in the world.

Source: WHO GTCR, 2023

Change in prevalence in selected countries

Trends in daily tobacco smoking among males (age 15+ yrs) in selected countries with the largest increase in prevalence

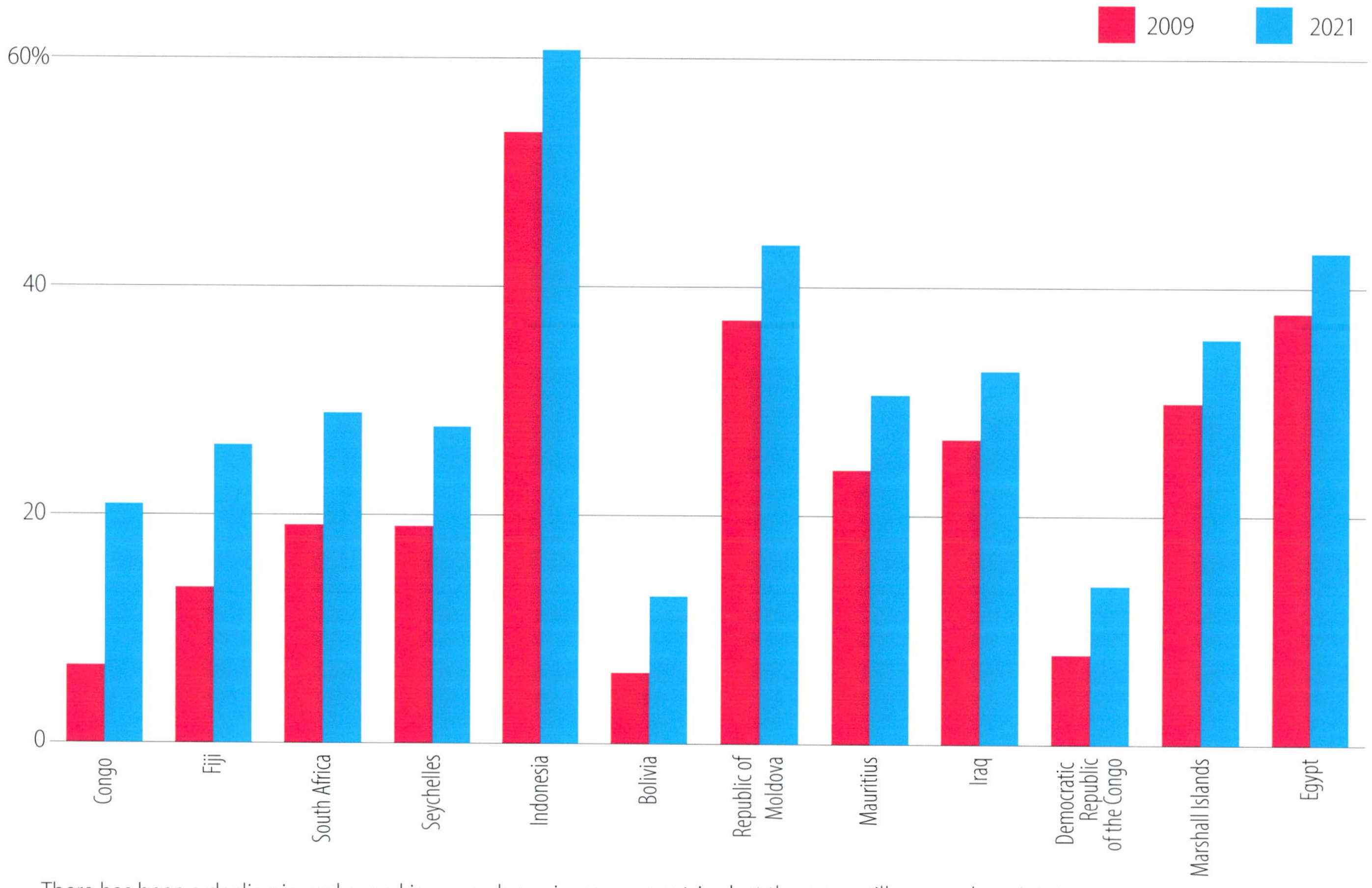

There has been a decline in male smoking prevalence in many countries but there are still some where it is increasing.

Source: GTCR 2011, 2023

Countries with the most smokers

Countries with the highest number of smokers (age 15+ yrs), in millions, 2019

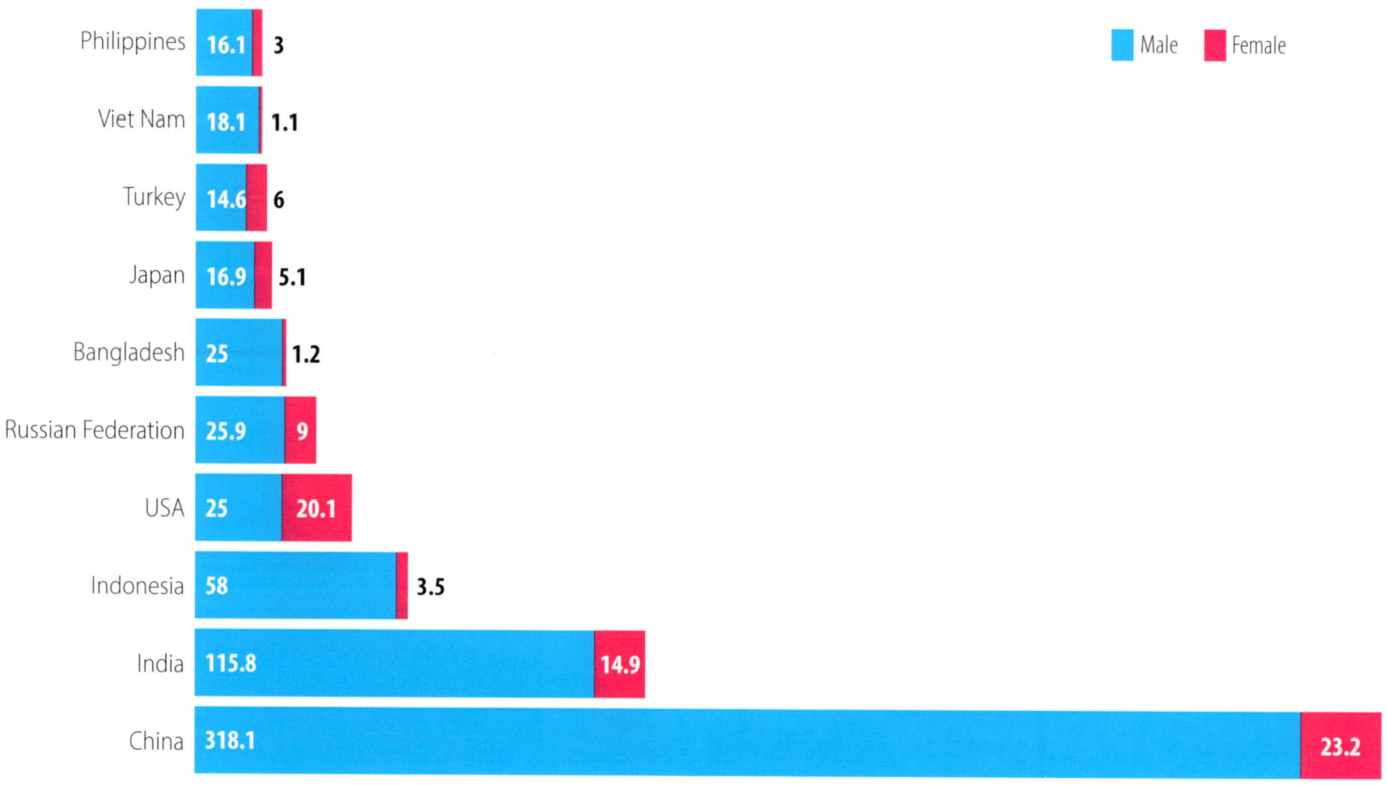

More than 500 million smokers live in three countries. One-third of all male smokers globally live in China.

Source: GBD, 2019

relatively moderate. Historically, smoking prevalence has been modest in most low-HDI countries, though this still translates into tens of millions of smokers. Female smoking prevalence in very high-HDI countries peaked a few decades later than the peak in male smoking, but it has remained relatively low or had only a moderate increase thus far in most low-, medium-, and high-HDI countries.

The earlier decreasing trend in smoking prevalence in most very high-HDI countries has stalled in recent years, however, and smoking prevalence has continued to rise or remain at high levels in many medium- or high-HDI countries. Since 1990, consumption per capita has declined in all WHO regions while, at the same time, the number of smokers has significantly increased in at least three (and possibly four), leading to greater overall consumption. Male smoking prevalence has increased in about one-third of medium- or high-HDI countries, while in almost all very high-HDI countries prevalence has either declined or remained unchanged. On the other hand, female smoking prevalence has increased in more than one-third of high-HDI countries and in about one-fifth of very-high HDI countries.

Notably, some countries – mostly in Africa – are experiencing increases in prevalence. In the future this trend is likely to occur in many others, especially low-HDI countries, due to income growth and increasing cigarette affordability as well as the tobacco industry's strategy of aggressive marketing in those countries. This trend can be reversed if governments implement stronger tobacco control policies, including raising taxes to increase the prices of tobacco products.

Another major concern is a recent increase in smoking prevalence among youth, particularly among females in several countries, in some of which smoking among adolescent females is now more common than among adult females or even adolescent males. Article 20 of the WHO Framework Convention on Tobacco Control obliges Parties to conduct surveillance on the magnitude, patterns, determinants, and consequences of tobacco use. From 2007 to 2020, however, about half of African countries and more than 40% of Eastern Mediterranean countries have regressed in their implementation of prevalence monitoring measures. Moreover, more than 70% of all countries with no recent monitoring data are in Africa. Effective monitoring at the national level must be a priority for governments, as this is essential for estimating the tobacco-related burden and evaluating the success of tobacco control policies.

Although tobacco use remains a major health issue worldwide, the declines in prevalence in countries with active tobacco control efforts demonstrate that we can reduce smoking with effective strategies.

26 October 2023

The above information is reprinted with kind permission from The Tobacco Atlas, Vital Strategies and Economics for Health at Johns Hopkins University.

www.tobaccoatlas.org

Risk Factors Map

Create a mind map showing the factors that can increase smoking in some countries. Include income growth, affordable cigarettes, aggressive marketing, weak monitoring, youth smoking and limited tobacco control policies.

The cultural power in a cigarette puff

Globally, rates of smoking are in decline. But in Indonesia, a cigarette is a measure of masculinity and hospitality. That makes it a habit hard to break.

By Christianez Ratna Kiruba

To see blue fire that flames up as high as five meters inside a volcanic crater, I trekked with a group of tourists on an overnight expedition to the Kawah Ijen National Park on the island of Java in Indonesia.

Kawah Ijen is known for its yellow sulphur deposits which produce the iconic blue fire flames. They can only be seen in the dark.

It was the only light we could see, aside from a glow from the cigarette held by my chain smoking guide.

In my 10 days in the country, I saw the same scene countless times: men chain-smoking beside their families, in markets, on buses, sometimes even while holding their children.

'My father was a smoker,' said the guide, whose name I'm withholding to protect his identity. 'Even as a toddler, I remember him holding me in one hand while holding a cigarette in the other.'

Globally, tobacco use remains a major public health challenge, though patterns vary widely.

The undisputed danger of smoking

Still holding a cigarette, my guide to the crater told how his wife recently miscarried twins. I stopped to ask if he smoked inside his house, and he replied yes.

A 2019 study showed exposure to cigarette smoke (also known as passive or secondhand smoking) was responsible for 14% of population attributable stillbirths in Indonesia. This means that 14% of stillbirths in Indonesia can be linked to this one risk factor.

According to a 2024 report from the World Health Organization, about 25% of people aged 15 or over in the European region smoke cigarettes. In Southeast Asia, a little over 26% of people use tobacco. There is a big gender gap in that number: It accounts for half of all males but only 14% of females.

Smoking remains the dominant form of tobacco use worldwide. Nearly 90% of smokers rely on cigarettes, which are linked to cancer, cardiovascular disease, respiratory illness and a significant burden of preventable deaths each year.

Indonesia, however, stands out even within the Southeast Asian region. With nearly 70% of adult men smoking – the highest percentage in the world – the country not only defies regional trends but also highlights a deeply entrenched cultural acceptance of cigarettes.

Unlike in many countries where smoking is increasingly seen as socially undesirable, in Indonesia it remains intertwined with masculinity, social etiquette and hospitality, making the epidemic as much a cultural challenge as a public health one.

The economic costs of tobacco addiction

The costs of this cultural acceptance are staggering. Smoking in Indonesia has been well established as a public health concern for the country. Smoking-related illness is reported to be as high as 93% in hospitalised Indonesian men according to a 2015 study.

A 2022 study showed that, in the year 2019, the economic cost of smoking-related illness – the costs of healthcare and lost productivity – was almost 1.5–2.5% of the gross domestic product of Indonesia. That's the data point used to measure the economic health of a country.

Passive smoking, however, also significantly plays a role in these figures, with nearly half of the recorded cancer cases in the country resulting from passive smoking.

In recent years, Indonesia has tried to reduce the number of smokers by adopting measures now common in many Western nations including increasing the age of purchase of cigarettes from 17 to 21 in 2024, banning the sale of cigarettes around educational institutions and increasing taxation on cigarettes.

However, a walk through Indonesian streets reveals that many teenagers under 21 have easy access to cigarettes even after the legal reform. The introduction of e-cigarettes has also increased smoking in Indonesian youth.

Curbing a collective habit

The reason for the failure of Indonesia to curb smoking is that Indonesian policy deals with cigarettes as a product, while the people view cigarettes as a cultural symbol.

A study about the beliefs and norms associated with smoking in Indonesian teenagers revealed that many teenage boys believed that they were 'Not a real man' if they did not smoke. There is also an ostracisation of non-smokers as effeminate men in Indonesia.

In some ways this mirrors the marketing of cigarettes in the United States for about 50 years. The iconic Marlboro Man, an image of a rugged cowboy that advertised Marlboro cigarettes, wasn't retired until 1999.

Furthermore, smoking has also found a way into becoming a part of good social etiquette in Indonesia. In local community and family events, hosts serve cigarettes to the attendees as a form of respect. This leads to about 70% of Indonesian homes being the sites of secondhand smoke exposure to non-smoking women and children.

Behavioural studies also show that Indonesian men use cigarettes as a status symbol – smoking expensive cigarettes shows that they are financially well-off.

The effect on a family's economic health

According to several studies, this acceptance of smoking as a household essential expenditure also competes directly with money spent on nutrition and other basic needs.

This shows that smoking has an impoverishing effect on Indonesian households. And even after recent price increases, Indonesian cigarettes are still cheaper than in most lower and middle-income countries. At least one study has found that raising the price of cigarettes could serve to worsen poverty rather than spur smokers to quit.

In contrast to the guide who took us to see the blue flames, Wisnu, a driver who took us to see some Balinese temples, said he has never smoked. Neither his father nor grandfather smoked and that's the reason, he said, that he never lit up a cigarette in his life.

'There needs to be a cultural overhaul in the acceptance of smoking as a tolerable habit,' Wisnu said. 'Every single person I have met that doesn't smoke, I have noticed that the common factor they have is a parent that didn't smoke as well.'

Studies back up Wisnu's theory. Young men who came from families with fathers who smoked or from families where smoking was accepted and tolerated went on to become smokers themselves.

Warning labels are not enough.

To break this intergenerational hold of smoking on Indonesian men, public health efforts must go beyond warning labels and taxation. They must reshape the cultural meaning of smoking itself.

This means creating a counter-narrative where cigarettes are no longer seen as symbols of camaraderie or manhood, but as markers of exploitation by the tobacco industry and threats to family wellbeing. Religion offers a compelling entry point for this cultural shift.

Indonesia is the world's largest Muslim-majority country, and its citizens often place high trust in religious authorities. If Islamic leaders across the country were mobilised to speak with one voice, linking tobacco use to neglect of one's duty to protect life and health, this could create a strong moral imperative to quit.

Public campaigns could pair this religious framing with stories of families harmed by smoking, making the message emotionally resonant as well as doctrinally sound.

Public campaigns must also elevate male role models – sports stars, musicians, politicians – who proudly reject smoking, reframing masculinity in terms other than lighting up a cigarette. Popular media, including films, television and social media influencers, should depict non-smoking as aspirational and smoking as outdated or socially irresponsible.

Where schools come in

Furthermore, school-based education should portray tobacco companies as predatory businesses targeting the poor and youth, thereby reframing smoking as an act of corporate manipulation rather than free choice.

Several countries have done this in the past. Thailand enacted the Non-Smokers' Health Protection Act in 1992, which declared that non-smokers have a protected right to clean air. This led to designated venues for smoking while protecting non-smoking areas. In Malaysia, in 1995, the National Fatwa Council declared smoking to be 'haram' (forbidden) in Islam due to its harmful health effects.

This religious edict has influenced public perception of smoking as a negative habit. South Korea has shown declining smoking rates, especially among men, over the years. And studies done in South Korea reveal that currently there is stigmatisation of smoking in the public consciousness of the country. Such a perception leads to more people attempting to quit.

These examples show that there are ways in which Indonesia can adapt to make smoking undesirable for its people.

Positive masculinity can be embraced by reframing men as protectors and providers who would never compromise their family's health or diminish household nutrition by spending on cigarettes. In that scenario, smoking shifts from a symbol of manhood to a betrayal of it.

This approach links masculinity to safeguarding children's lungs, ensuring food on the table and embodying responsibility – turning smoke-free living into a proud badge of honour.

Questions to consider

1. Why does smoking seem to be so pervasive in Indonesia when the rest of the world is kicking the habit?
2. How do you get people to change behaviour that is culturally acceptable?
3. If you were a health minister of your country what policies or laws regarding cigarettes would you impose if able?

15 September 2025

Teenagers as young as 12 prescribed nicotine gum on NHS

Number of children using e-cigarettes in schools is soaring.

By Matthew Davis

Teenagers as young as 12 are being prescribed nicotine gum amid soaring numbers of children using e-cigarettes.

Doctors are issuing hundreds of prescriptions for nicotine patches and gum to addict teenagers, many of whom are still too young to legally smoke.

The disclosure comes at a time when the number of children smoking cigarettes has declined but the numbers using vapes, which can contain nicotine, has soared in recent years.

Last year, almost 1,300 prescriptions were issued to teenagers who had gone to their doctor for help to beat their nicotine cravings.

The statistics show that last year children as young as 12 were given help to wean them off.

Lee Fernandes, lead therapist at addiction specialist the UKAT Group, said: 'Children as young as 12 being addicted to nicotine is of real concern as it can lead to developmental abnormalities, stunting their ability to learn and play.

Vaping admissions set to hit record high

Number of hospital admissions for those aged 0 to 19 per year, England

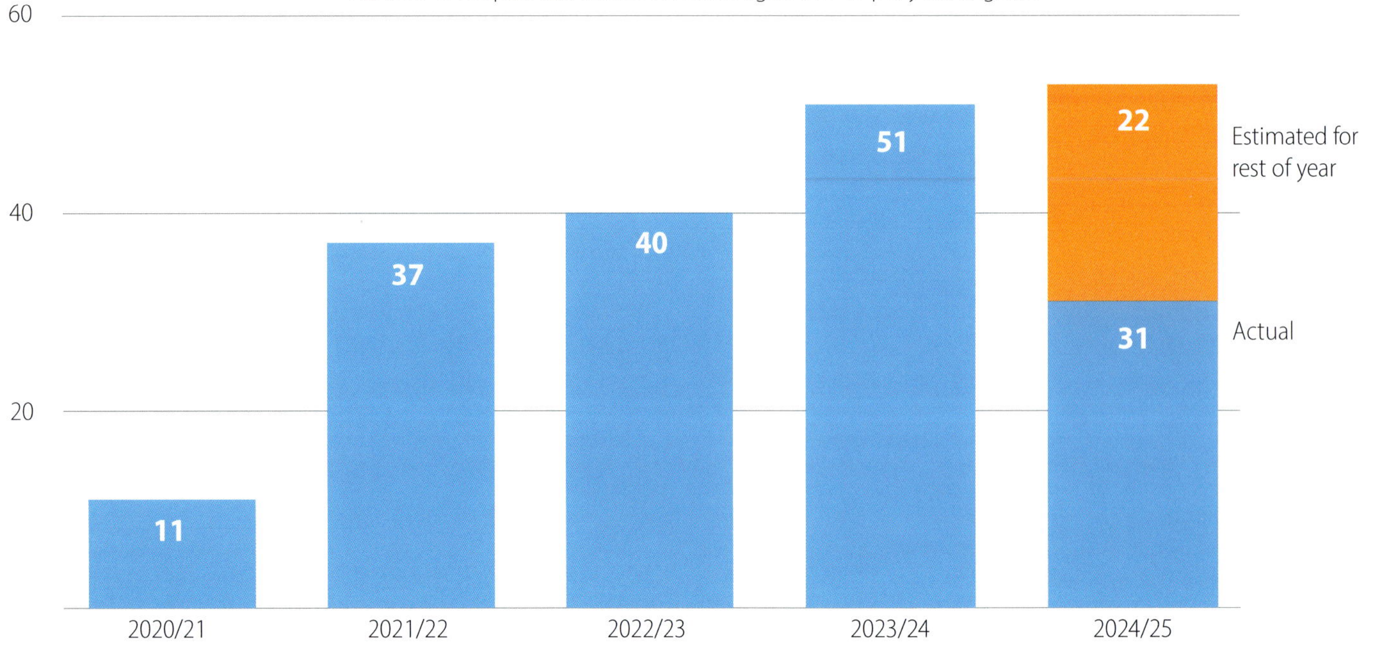

Source: 2024/25 data up to October 31 . Figure assumes similar rate of admissions for rest of the year

'Ultimately, what these figures tell us is that there is not enough education in schools about the dangers of smoking, and we'd urge the Government to do something about this.'

Addiction issues

Nicotine gum costs the NHS anything from £2 to £10 per prescription, depending on how many items are issued, while the patches can cost as much as £25.

It means that every year thousands of pounds of NHS cash is being spent on helping children fight nicotine addictions.

NHS officials have said it is money well spent if the treatment helps children beat their addiction to cigarettes and dodge the associated health problems linked to a lifetime of smoking.

Nicotine patches are used to try to help wean people off their addiction to the drug, with a course typically lasting ten weeks.

The chewing gums and lozenges are used to help fight off the immediate craving for a cigarette, with patients told not to take more than 15 per day.

In 2023, there were a total of 246 of these prescriptions issued to under-16s. It is illegal to sell cigarettes or vapes to those under the age of 18 in the UK.

Figures from the NHS show a fall in the number of children using cigarettes, but an increase in the amount of those who have tried e-cigarettes.

The survey found just 2% of 11- to 15-year-olds were current smokers, although 11% had admitted being smokers at some point.

On vaping, 9% of pupils said they were currently using e-cigarettes, however this figure rose to 22% among 15-year-old girls.

Proposed legislation

Prof Sanjay Agrawal, NHS England national speciality advisor for tobacco dependency, said: 'It's terrible to see young people, especially those under-age, getting hold of cigarettes.

'We know that 200 to 300 young people each day experiment with or start smoking – and one in two adult long-term smokers will die from tobacco-related disease.

'This is why we support the proposed legislation as part of the Tobacco and Vapes Bill, which will raise the age of sale so that young people will never be able to legally purchase tobacco in the UK.

'For those who become addicted to tobacco, we want to do as much as we can to help them quit. NHS programmes, such as licensed nicotine replacement therapies helping hundreds of teenagers and young people each year to stop smoking, live healthier lives and avoid becoming ill.'

A government spokesman said: 'This government is not prepared to stand by and allow a new generation of kids to get hooked on nicotine. Our landmark Tobacco and Vapes Bill will protect children and young people by creating the first smoke-free generation.

'The biggest public health intervention in a generation, the Bill will save thousands of lives, and we will also ban the sale of single-use vapes from June.'

4 January 2025

Questions

1. Why are some teenagers being prescribed nicotine gum or patches?
2. How young were some children receiving help for nicotine addiction?
3. What has happened to cigarette smoking among children in recent years?
4. What has happened to vaping among children in recent years?
5. How many prescriptions were issued to teenagers last year to help with nicotine cravings?
6. Why did Lee Fernandes describe nicotine addiction in 12-year-olds as a serious concern?
7. Why do NHS officials argue that spending money on nicotine replacement treatments can be worthwhile?
8. What percentage of 11- to 15-year-olds were current smokers?
9. What percentage of 15-year-old girls were currently using e-cigarettes?
10. What is the aim of the proposed Tobacco and Vapes Bill?

Should the NHS Help?

Write a short balanced response to this question: should the NHS spend money helping children quit nicotine? Include one argument about cost, one argument about health, and one argument about preventing future harm. End with your own view, supported by evidence from the article.

Nicotine Support Flow Chart

Create a flow chart showing how a young person might move from trying vapes or cigarettes to needing help for nicotine cravings. Include addiction, cravings, nicotine replacement treatments, support from doctors, and the aim of quitting.

Graphic warnings on tobacco products are losing their impact – here are 5 ways to improve them

An article from The Conversation.

By Janet Hoek, Professor in Public Health, University of Otago, Andrew Waa, Associate Professor in Public Health, University of Otago, Lani Teddy, Research Fellow in Public Health, University of Otago and Philip Gendall, Senior Research Fellow in Marketing, University of Otago

Large pictorial warning labels on smoked tobacco products typically feature confronting images of the harmful health outcomes of smoking. Pictures of diseased lungs, gangrene and mouth decay aim to elicit strong emotional responses that reduce the appeal and acceptability of smoking, particularly among young people.

Warning labels also aim to increase knowledge of the many risks smoking poses. Plain packaging increases the attention paid to warning labels and reduces pack appeal, brand loyalty and product perceptions.

However, like any marketing campaign, warning labels on tobacco products need regular updating so they continue to attract attention and communicate the latest research evidence. Maintaining the same images risks 'wear-out', when people lose interest in campaign images and messages, or counter argue these.

Our recent work found existing tobacco warnings have lost impact. Study participants had created cognitive defences and exempted themselves from the risks shown.

While some still found images of diseased body parts shocking, others did not consider the illustrated risks personally relevant and thought warnings lacked credibility.

Our findings raise the important question of how we can make on-pack warnings more impactful and effective. Our new study addresses this question by exploring the lived experiences of people who smoke.

Creating more effective warnings

Many find smoking imposes a heavy financial burden on them, and others worry about the impact smoking has on whānau (families).

Others resent the hold nicotine addiction has over them and feel concerned that young people may want to adopt the behaviour they see modelled by adults who smoke.

Working with a graphic artist, we developed images and messages to represent the ideas we had heard.

After extensive review with people who smoke, we identified three potential warning themes for final testing: the cost of smoking, smoking's impact on family, and the health risks presented in a more empathetic way (by featuring people rather than diseased body parts).

Using a choice study, we examined how well warnings representing these themes prompted thoughts of quitting compared to a novel graphic health warning showing a mouth cancer.

We found two different groups among our sample of people who smoke: one responded more strongly to warning labels emphasising the cost of smoking and its effect on families than to the graphic warning we used as a control; the other group reacted more strongly to an empathetic health warning than to the control.

5 ways to improve on-pack warnings

1. We need warnings that reflect people's experiences of smoking, recognise smoking's various harms, and understand that people who smoke are not a homogenous group. While most people who smoke regret smoking and hope to quit, they are at different life stages, have different backgrounds and interests, and respond to different stimuli.

   For example, the cost-of-living crisis means warnings reinforcing the cost of smoking, the opportunities forgone and the impacts on others may be more motivating for some people than graphic health warnings.

2. We should think more creatively about the health harm from smoking. We found images of children losing a parent to an illness caused by smoking created strong emotional connections, as did images of adults smoking near children.

   This approach, which illustrates how smoking causes emotional and physical harm to others, was at least as effective as the graphic mouth cancer image we used as a control.

3. We should consider the impact of warnings on emotions. Early graphic warnings aimed to arouse fear, in the belief it would galvanise attempts to quit. However, people who smoke also experience regret and shame, which may be more motivating than fear.

4. We need to balance negative emotions, which may stigmatise people and lead them to feel powerless, by introducing pack inserts with positive messages. Our work found that offering helpful advice and outlining the benefits of quitting inspired participants and could support attempts to quit.

5. We need to refresh and rotate warnings much more often. We suggest new warnings should be introduced every six months and that no warning should run for longer than a year.

   On-pack pictorial warnings are a proven best-practice approach to encouraging smoking cessation. However, failure to introduce new and more diverse warnings has compromised the impact these have.

Given people who smoke consume, on average, ten cigarettes a day, on-pack warnings have high potential exposure. We should be making this measure as effective as possible and embed it within a comprehensive strategy that will reduce tobacco's addictiveness, appeal and accessibility.

14 September 2025

THE CONVERSATION

The above information is reprinted with kind permission from The Conversation.

www.theconversation.com

Warning Label Review

Read the article and list three reasons why old tobacco warning labels may stop being effective. Include ideas such as wear-out, people thinking the warnings do not apply to them, and lack of credibility. Then explain which reason you think is the biggest problem and why.

Design a Better Poster

Create a poster that encourages people to quit smoking. Base it on one of the warning themes in the article: cost, family impact, or health risks shown in a more human and empathetic way. Include a strong slogan, one image idea, and two short facts or messages that would make the poster persuasive.

Compare the Warning Themes

In pairs, compare these three warning approaches: graphic health images, cost-of-smoking messages, and family-impact messages. For each one, write one strength and one weakness. Finish by deciding which type of warning would be most effective for teenagers or young adults, using evidence from the article.

Warning Label Diamond 9

In small groups, create a Diamond 9 ranking of what makes a tobacco warning effective. Use ideas such as strong image, clear message, personal relevance, emotional impact, up-to-date evidence, practical advice, family focus, cost focus and regular updates. Put the most important feature at the top and justify your top three choices.

Fear or Support?

Which is more effective: shocking health images or supportive quitting advice? Choose one and explain your answer using evidence from the article.

Scotland's smoking ban turns 20 – it cut secondhand smoke exposure by 96%, but the job isn't finished yet

An article from The Conversation.

By Sean Semple, Professor, Institute for Social Marketing, University of Stirling & Rachel O'Donnell, Associate Professor, University of Stirling

At 6am on a quiet Sunday morning 20 years ago today, Scotland became the first UK nation to ban smoking in enclosed public spaces. It was a landmark moment in public health policy, and new research shows just how much has changed since.

Exposure to secondhand tobacco smoke has fallen by 96% in Scotland since the legislation came into force on March 26 2006. But our new study, published in the journal *Tobacco Induced Diseases*, reveals that nearly one in four people are still being exposed to tobacco smoke in settings the law does not fully cover. This raises the question of what it will take to finish what the ban started.

The Smoking, Health and Social Care (Scotland) Act 2005 made it illegal to smoke inside bars, restaurants, public transport and almost all workplaces. While there had been much lobbying for exemptions for bars on the basis of size, existing ventilation, or whether or not they also sold food, the law, when it was finally introduced, was comprehensive and simple.

Despite the scale of the change, adoption was rapid and without much dispute. It is now inconceivable that we could ever return to a time when people had to breathe high concentrations of a known carcinogen as they chatted in bars, ate dinner or sat at their workplace desk.

We should take time today to celebrate the impact of the smoking ban. Scotland led the way in the UK and showed it could be done. It also generated extensive evidence through a seven-study evaluation programme that covered everything from hospital admissions for heart attack (reduced by 17% after legislation), to air quality in bars (improved by 86%), to qualitative work examining changes in behaviour, attitudes and social norms.

That detailed and extensive evidence would go on to influence tobacco control policy decisions around the globe for years to come.

Our new analysis examines how Scotland's exposure to secondhand tobacco smoke has changed in the 20 years since the smoking ban. We used the annual Scottish Health Survey, which gathers data from about 6,000 people across the country, and includes a group of participants who

provide a sample of saliva. From this saliva, it is possible to determine the amount of nicotine that someone has inhaled in the past couple of days.

Our analysis shows that adult non-smokers now inhale 96% less nicotine than they did before the ban. Scotland has switched from a nation where seven out of eight non-smokers inhaled other people's smoke, to a country where three out of four breathe no measurable secondhand tobacco smoke today.

And the progress hasn't been limited to the settings where the law applies. Our study also provides an analysis of a survey question included since 2012, when people were asked about whether they permit smoking inside their own home. The percentage of homes where smoking is allowed has more than halved in a little over a decade – from 25% to under 10% in 2024.

We've made fantastic progress in tackling secondhand smoke exposure in such a short space of time, and it is tempting to see this as a problem solved. But dig deeper and there is a sting in the tail.

The data we present shows that nearly one in four adult non-smokers still breathe secondhand tobacco smoke, and that this figure has been relatively static in the past decade. Workers in many sectors still report they are exposed to other people's smoke – from those serving in outdoor hospitality settings, to the healthcare workers who provide assistance to people in their own homes.

And as our study reports, we still have about one in ten homes where smoking takes place indoors. While we've seen major progress and reductions in that figure, the change also masks a growing inequality. When we look at smoking in the home by deprivation, we see that more than a fifth of households in the most deprived postcodes allow smoking indoors compared with just 2% in the most affluent areas – that inequality gap has doubled since 2012.

Unfinished business

So where next? The Tobacco And Vapes Bill is progressing through the parliament and will provide new powers to extend smoke-free spaces to other settings in the UK.

Consultation on how to use these powers has already started, with options to provide protection in a whole range of outdoor and indoor spaces including playgrounds, at school entrances and in outdoor hospitality settings.

Tackling secondhand smoke in the remaining workplaces and homes where exposure continues to take place is a priority.

As we celebrate 20 years of smoke-free enclosed public spaces in Scotland, it is worth reflecting that the benefits have been extensive. For you it may be that you avoided a hospital admission for a heart attack or stroke, or your child didn't need that GP appointment for their asthma or glue ear (a common ear infection in children).

Or perhaps it was just the simple joy of not having to wash your hair to get rid of the stink of smoke when you come home from a night out. Whatever your reason, it is little wonder that smoke-free spaces are viewed as one of the most important public health achievements of the first part of the 21st century.

25 March 2026

Who Is Protected?

List five groups who may benefit from smoking bans, such as children, workers, pregnant women, people with asthma, and non-smokers. For each group, explain one way a ban could help them.

Smoke-Free Spaces

Create a ranking of places where smoking should be banned, from most important to least important. Include schools, playgrounds, hospitals, parks, beaches and outdoor restaurants. Explain your top two choices.

How do I stop smoking?

Discover the tools and options available to help you stop smoking, including information on free local stop smoking services – you're more likely to stop for good with their advice and support.

What can help with giving up smoking?

Stopping smoking is the best thing you can do for your health, and there are a range of tools and services to help you succeed.

To give you the best chance of success, get support from your free local stop smoking services.

You can also use stop smoking tools such as:

- Prescription medicines
- Nicotine replacement therapy (NRT)
- E-cigarettes.

How you choose to stop is up to you, so find the method that works for you. Giving up smoking for good might take a few attempts or involve trying different methods. We know it can be hard to stop smoking, but keep trying.

Nicotine is the chemical that makes smoking so addictive. These stop smoking tools are designed to help you control cravings for nicotine. Your stop smoking advisor, doctor or pharmacist can give you advice on which tool or combination of tools could work for you.

Whichever tool you're using, make sure you follow their advice and the manufacturer's instructions. All the tools are

What are my stop smoking options?

You don't have to go it alone, there are tools and services to help you succeed.

For the best chance of success, get support from your free local stop smoking services.

Prescription medicines

Switching to e-cigarettes

Nicotine replacement therapy (NRT) like patches, gum and sprays

Source: Cancer Research UK

most effective when you use them with advice and support from a stop smoking service.

Stop smoking medicines

- Stop smoking medicines can reduce your cravings and help with nicotine withdrawal symptoms.
- You need a prescription for these medicines.
- Ask your doctor about the options for stop smoking medicines.

Nicotine replacement therapy (NRT)

- NRT gives you nicotine to satisfy your cravings without the harmful chemicals in tobacco smoke.
- There are lots of different types including nasal sprays, gums and patches.
- NRT is available on prescription from a doctor or free local stop smoking service, or to buy over the counter at a pharmacy or supermarket.

Vapes/e-cigarettes

- E-cigarettes ('vapes') are electronic devices that deliver nicotine in a vapour that you inhale.
- They can satisfy your cravings but don't contain tobacco, so they're far less harmful than smoking.
- You can buy them from specialist vape shops, some pharmacies, supermarkets and convenience stores.

What's the best way to stop smoking?

The best way to stop smoking is using a combination of stop smoking treatment and specialist help from free local stop smoking services. You're more likely to give up smoking for good with their advice and support. Stop smoking services are free to use and offer a range of help including:

- Free 1 to 1 or group support sessions where a trained advisor can support you to stop smoking.
- Providing stop smoking treatment to help control cravings.
- Advice on switching to e-cigarettes.

Stop smoking services may be delivered in person or online. You can contact your free local service for details.

If you don't want to use a stop smoking service or you're not able to, you can also get help with stopping smoking from:

- The NHS Quit Smoking app for smartphones
- The NHS Smokefree online community forum on Facebook

What happens when I stop smoking?

Nicotine withdrawal symptoms

There are lifelong benefits to stopping smoking, but it can be difficult at first. The nicotine in tobacco is addictive, so going without it can cause uncomfortable withdrawal symptoms such as:

- Feeling depressed, anxious, irritable, restless or hungry
- Poor concentration
- Poor sleep at night
- Urges to smoke
- Feeling sick
- Feeling unwell
- Headaches

Everyone's different, so there is no guaranteed timeline for smoking withdrawal symptoms. Symptoms usually peak during the first few days after your last cigarette and then get easier over two to four weeks. If you normally have a cough caused by smoking, you might notice this gets worse for a while when you stop, while your body gets used to not smoking any more. Stop smoking tools can ease withdrawal symptoms and specialist support can help you to cope with them until they pass.

Will I gain weight if I stop smoking?

Some people who smoke may gain weight after stopping. A review of studies found that people who stopped smoking had gained around 4kg a year after stopping. But not everyone gains weight when they stop smoking, and the evidence does not show increased weight in the long term for people who stop smoking.

It's understandable that some people may be concerned about gaining weight. But, if you smoke, stopping is the best thing you can do for your health. You can talk to your doctor or nurse if you have any questions about your weight, and we have top tips for keeping a healthy weight on our website.

What are the benefits of stopping smoking?

It's never too late to stop smoking. There are many benefits to stopping smoking, from improving your physical and mental health to saving money:

- ✅ Cut your cancer risk. Stopping smoking reduces your risk of at least 16 types of cancer, including lung cancer.
- ✅ Lower your risk of lung and heart conditions. Including heart attack, stroke and chronic obstructive pulmonary disease (COPD).
- ✅ Feel healthier. Stopping smoking could help you feel better in your daily life. Many people report breathing more easily after giving up and that they have more energy.
- ✅ Improve your mental wellbeing. Potential positive feelings from smoking a cigarette only last for a short time. Stopping smoking can lower depression, anxiety, and stress in the long term.
- ✅ Protect your friends and family. There is no safe level of secondhand smoke, and passive smoking is particularly dangerous for children and those who are pregnant.
- ✅ Healthier appearance. Smoking can damage the skin and make it look grey, but stopping can help reverse this. Giving up smoking also stops your teeth becoming stained.
- ✅ Save money. Smoking can cost thousands of pounds a year. What else could you use that money for?

Top tips for stopping smoking for good

We know that stopping smoking can be hard. Smoking can be part of a well-established routine, which can be difficult to break.

But thousands of people stop smoking every year in the UK, and you can do it too! Here are our top tips to get you started.

Decide when to do it

Making a plan increases your chances of doing something. Decide on a date when you will stop smoking and stick to it.

Be prepared

Think about what could get in the way of you stopping smoking. For situations that you might find difficult, plan what actions you'll take to help yourself. For example if you are socialising with friends who smoke.

Ask for help

Although it is hard, you don't need to go it alone. Talk to your free local stop smoking service or your doctor. They can give you help and advice.

Tell people you're stopping

Friends and family can then support and encourage you and celebrate your smokefree milestones.

Keep trying

It takes most people a few tries before they manage to stop smoking for good. If you don't succeed at first, think about what worked and what didn't, and what you could do differently next time. Your stop smoking service, doctor or pharmacy can help you find a method that works for you.

Focus on your motivation

Remember why you decided to stop smoking and what the personal benefits are for you – try leaving sticky notes for yourself or set reminders on your phone.

Change your routine

If you're used to smoking at certain times, try doing things differently to break the link between a certain time or activity and you smoking. For example, if you normally smoke after a meal, try going for a walk or doing something you enjoy instead.

Keep your mind and hands busy

Even with stop smoking tools, you'll probably still feel the urge to smoke sometimes. Try doing something else to distract you, like exercising, watching TV or reading. It may help to hold something in the hand that normally holds your cigarette.

How do I stop smoking with nicotine replacement therapy (NRT)?

There are lots of different types of NRT, and they can all increase your chances of stopping smoking. Your stop smoking service, pharmacist or doctor can help you choose your NRT and advise you on how to use it and for how long.

- Nicotine patches give you a steady supply of nicotine to help reduce cravings and withdrawal symptoms throughout the day.
- Products like nicotine gum, lozenges and spray give you a quicker, shorter dose of nicotine.

Everyone's different, so find the NRT product that works for you. You can combine more than one product, which is particularly effective. For example, you might use long-acting patches with a shorter-acting type to 'top up' your nicotine when you need it. Whichever type or combination you use, make sure you're using enough to help with your withdrawal symptoms and cravings. Nicotine doesn't cause cancer, so NRT is safe to use for as long as you need it.

Can vaping help me to quit smoking?

Research shows using e-cigarettes (vaping) can help people to stop smoking.

This is because they allow you to breathe in nicotine in a vapour, relieving cravings. Vaping can also feel similar to smoking, like holding a cigarette and breathing in.

Although more research is needed into their long-term effects, studies so far have found that legal e-cigarettes are far less harmful than smoking. This is because they do not contain tobacco, which is responsible for the harmful effects of smoking cigarettes.

E-cigarettes should only be used to help you stop smoking, or to stop you going back to tobacco. If you have never smoked, you shouldn't use e-cigarettes.

If you want to use an e-cigarette to stop smoking, your stop smoking service, pharmacist or doctor can advise you. Here are some tips that can help you to use an e-cigarette to stop smoking:

- Don't get caught out – remember to charge your e-cigarette and bring refills when you leave the house.
- Use the right nicotine strength for you – if you find your e-cigarette is not relieving your cravings, you may not be using a high enough concentration of nicotine in your e-liquid.
- Experiment – there are lots of different types of devices and flavours of e-liquid. Find what works for you.

Are there medicines to help me stop smoking?

There are prescription medicines, such as varenicline and bupropion, that can help you stop smoking by reducing cravings and helping with withdrawal symptoms. Ask your doctor about the option of stop smoking medicines.

19 June 2023

www.cancerresearchuk.org

Quit Plan

Create a simple quit plan for someone who wants to stop smoking. Include a quit date, one support service they could use, one stop smoking tool, and two ways to deal with cravings.

Benefits Ranking

Rank five benefits of quitting smoking from most important to least important. Choose from better breathing, lower cancer risk, improved mental wellbeing, saving money, protecting others and healthier appearance. Explain your top choice..

Top 5 mental health benefits of quitting smoking

In this article we'll share some of the lesser known benefits of quitting smoking – the benefits to your mental health and wellbeing!

The physical health benefits of stopping smoking are quite well-known, but did you know these five mental health benefits of quitting?

1. You'll feel less stressed

Many believe that smoking helps relieve stress but the opposite is actually true. Smoking and stress are linked and numerous studies show that smoking increases anxiety and tension.

When you're craving nicotine, this creates feelings of stress in your body. The longer you go without a cigarette, the more irritable you'll become.

Smoking relieves these nicotine cravings, making you feel instantly relaxed. But don't be fooled, it's not the smoking helping you to relax, as many believe – it's the nicotine withdrawal creating the stress in the first place. That's why this relief is only temporary and the stress will quickly build again, alongside your craving.

Scientific studies show that after quitting, your stress levels will lower and you'll feel less stressed than someone who smokes.

Although dealing with stress can be a reason for not wanting to quit, there is lots of support available to help you through your quitting journey with many ways of handling the stresses and strains of life much more effectively. Using nicotine replacement therapy – like patches and gum – can be a great way of relieving those cravings without smoking.

2. Feel happier

Smoking affects the chemistry of the brain and can act as a depressant. Research shows that smokers who stopped smoking for six weeks or more are happier than those who carry on smoking. Even better, the evidence suggests that quitting can be as effective as anti-depressants in reducing depression and anxiety.

For people with mental health conditions, like anxiety and depression, stopping smoking is likely to make you feel much calmer and more positive, improving your overall quality of life and happiness levels.

3. Take back control

Having a sense of control over your life makes you feel better. The more you perceive yourself to be in control the greater your sense of wellbeing and happiness.

When you smoke your addiction controls your life.

As well as taking over your thoughts, smoking can take vast amounts of time out of your day. Even shopping for cigarettes or looking for somewhere to smoke and going outside for a cigarette takes up time.

Stopping smoking puts you back in the driving seat.

Smoking will no longer control your daily thoughts and activities. You'll be free to chose how to spend your time and you'll be able to do things your way.

This feeling of being back in control can improve your mental wellbeing. Former smokers tell us how liberated and free they feel after giving up.

If you want to take back control of your life – maybe it's time to quit for good?

4. Reduce your financial worries

Money worries can lead to mental health issues such as stress, anxiety and depression.

With the current price of a packet of 20 cigarettes anywhere between £9 – £12, the cost of smoking has never been more expensive. Add to that the indirect costs such as potential loss of earnings if you're poorly and the financial burden of smoking can squeeze your budget to the max.

Quitting puts more money in your pocket instantly and these savings quickly add up. Use our cost savings calculator to see just how much you could save each month.

Very quickly you'll be able to use your savings on special treats or just helping your monthly budget go that little bit further.

5. Enjoy a better quality of life

Your physical and mental health are strongly linked to the quality of your life.

The happier and healthier you feel – the better your quality of life will be.

Smoking is the leading cause of preventable death and illness in the UK. Every year around 78,000 people in the UK die from smoking and it increases your risk of developing more than 50 serious health conditions including cancer.

Within two to 12 weeks of stopping smoking, your blood circulation improves making physical activity such as walking and running much easier. Your immune system also improves making it easier to fight off colds and flu.

As well as making you happier and healthier, stopping smoking will also help you save the money you would have spent on buying cigarettes. These factors will all contribute towards you enjoying a much better quality of life.

Where to get help to quit smoking?

Get personalised support to quit smoking from your Local Stop Smoking Service, GP or pharmacist. Or call the NHS Stop Smoking helpline free on 0300 123 1044.

If you currently take any medication (including antidepressants), talk to your GP before you stop smoking as your dosage may need to be monitored or reduced. This is because smoking can affect how some medications work.

www.makesmokinghistory.co.uk

Should I quit smoking cold turkey?

Some people try to quit smoking using only their willpower, without any extra help like nicotine replacement products or nicotine-free medicines. This is called going cold turkey.

But quitting smoking cold turkey can be really tough, because your body may have become dependent on nicotine over time.

In this article, you'll learn about smoking addiction, find out how dependent you are, and learn how support options can help you quit for good.

What is addiction?

Addiction means two things:

1. being physically and mentally dependent on something
2. that dependency causing harm

For example, if you need coffee every morning, you might be dependent on caffeine. But since it does not cause harm, it is not really an addiction.

What is dependence?

Dependence happens when someone feels like they need to use a substance regularly, either to feel 'normal', or to avoid feeling uncomfortable.

How do you develop a dependence on smoking?

Dependence develops when smoking becomes linked to your daily routines. Your body and mind may start expecting to smoke at certain times, like when you:

- wake up
- go for a walk
- wait for the bus

Because smoking also damages your health in many ways, it's known as an addiction.

Are you addicted to smoking?

There are some easy questions you can ask yourself to get a better idea of your level of dependence on smoking.

? How soon after waking up do you have your first cigarette?

If you smoke within 30 minutes of waking, it could mean you have a stronger dependence on cigarettes.

? Do you find it hard not to smoke in places where it's not allowed, like inside a cafe or a shop?

If you answered yes, this suggests you may have a stronger dependence on smoking.

? Which cigarette would be the hardest for you to give up?

If the first cigarette of the day is the toughest to give up, it is a sign of stronger dependence.

Did you know?

The younger you are when you start smoking, the more likely it is that you will be dependent on it later in life.

? How many cigarettes do you smoke in a day?

The more cigarettes you smoke daily, the more likely it is that you are dependent.

? Do you find yourself smoking more in the mornings?

If you smoke more often in the mornings, it is a sign of stronger dependence.

? Do you still smoke even when you are unwell in bed?

If this sounds like you, it suggests a higher level of dependence.

? If someone offers you a cigarette, how likely are you to say no?

If you find it hard to refuse a cigarette, you might be more dependent than you realise.

If any of these questions suggest you have a stronger dependence on smoking, then quitting may be harder than you think.

Although willpower is important, getting expert support and using stop smoking products will boost your chances of success.

> **Top tip**
>
> Combining nicotine-free medicine, like varenicline, with NRTs makes you over 5 times more likely to quit smoking for good!

What happens when you quit smoking

Smoking tobacco for many years means your brain gets used to the nicotine hit. This is why you feel like you need to smoke more often to feel good.

When you stop smoking, you may feel:

- a strong urge to smoke
- irritable or restless
- tense or low in mood.

These withdrawal symptoms can make quitting feel tough. That's why willpower alone is often not enough.

Research shows that using stop-smoking products and getting expert support can help you stay on track.

Make quitting easier with stop-smoking products

There are many stop-smoking products you can use to help you quit.

Nicotine-free medicines

Some treatments can help you quit smoking by blocking the effects of nicotine in your brain, so smoking feels less enjoyable.

These are called nicotine-free medicines. You can get these medicines through a prescription from your GP. Your local Stop Smoking service can also advise and give you a much better chance of quitting for good..

Nicotine replacement therapies (NRTs)

Other treatments give your body lower doses of nicotine, in a safer way. Nicotine replacement therapies (NRTs) like patches or gum help with cravings and withdrawal.

For the best results, combine slow-acting and fast-acting NRTs. A slow-acting nicotine patch provides steady relief all day, while fast-acting options like spray, gum, or lozenges help with sudden cravings.

Nicotine vapes

The routines and rituals of smoking can be hard to stop, but vaping can help you gradually let go of these while reducing the health risks of smoking cigarettes.

Some people find vaping helpful because the hand-to-mouth action is like smoking and gives similar sensations to smoking.

Get support

Quitting is much easier with the right support. Expert advisers at your local Stop Smoking Service offer free advice and help.

They can recommend NRTs and give you guidance on vaping. These advisers are trained professionals, and many are ex-smokers so they understand the challenges of quitting.

There are lots of other ways to get support too. Explore your support options to find what works best for you.

Download the free NHS Quit Smoking app

Use the NHS Quit Smoking app to help you quit smoking and start breathing more easily.

The app allows you to:

- track your progress
- see how much you're saving
- get daily support

Once you reach 28 days smoke-free, you're much more likely to quit for good!

You can overcome your smoking addiction

When you're dependant on smoking, quitting can be hard. But there are ways to make it easier and you don't have to do it on your own.

There are many proven products that can help you through the tough days, and support can really boost your chances.

Stopping smoking is one of the best things you can do for your health, so don't be afraid to try different ways to reach your goal!

www.nhs.uk

> **Quit Smoking Poster**
>
> Design a poster that encourages people to stop smoking. Include a clear slogan, at least three practical tips for quitting, and two benefits of giving up, such as better health or saving money. Make your poster supportive and motivating, and use colour, layout and images to help the message stand out.

> **Helping a Friend Quit**
>
> Write a short, supportive message to a friend who wants to quit smoking. Include two practical tips, one reason to keep going, and one way you could support them.

'I'm so glad I stopped when I did' - Mum and daughter urge others to quit smoking

Wendy and Amy have both successfully stubbed out the habit after life-changing experiences.

By Deborah Hall

Two former smokers are the faces of a major new campaign to inspire the region's 562,000 smokers to make a quit attempt. Mother and daughter Wendy and Amy Robinson are helping to lead the 'Turn the Corner' campaign, with the powerful message that every cigarette takes 20 minutes off your life.

The campaign, which launches today (Wednesday, April 8) features Wendy, 53, of Cleethorpes, and mum-to-be Amy, of Hull, who have both successfully quit smoking after life-changing experiences. Wendy quit after sadly losing her mum to the progressive lung disease, chronic obstructive pulmonary disease (COPD) so that daughter Amy would never have to go through the same experience.

With support from her local stop-smoking service, she quit using an inhalator and patches but unfortunately, she was later diagnosed with kidney cancer caused by smoking. The cancer was removed but the following year she was told she had lung cancer, also caused by smoking, and needed further surgery.

She said: 'I felt bad on my family and when I could see my husband crying, I'd think I don't want to lose him – it's not the surgery that upset me but thinking of my husband and daughter. I'm just so glad I stopped smoking when I did.'

Wendy said she felt she was turning the negative she had experienced into the positive by helping other people, through the campaign. 'I am here to tell the story,' she said, 'thank goodness I stopped smoking nine years ago.'

Wendy has lost three-and-a-half stonet since her lung surgery and 'never felt better'. She said stopping smoking was a 'life-changer' and urged people to 'get help, it's out there.'

Amy also smoked but after seeing what her mum went through, and finding out she was pregnant, she also decided to quit. Amy said: 'Seeing my mum go through kidney and then lung cancer was horrible.

'I thought, if she can stop smoking after 34 years, then I can quit too. And then finding out I was pregnant was a big motivator to keep going and stay quit.'

Amy's first baby is due in just over three weeks. She said it was 'surreal, really' to be helping to lead the quit-smoking initiative with her mum.

'If you'd have said five years ago I'd have been doing something like this, I'd have said "no way". I'd never been a heavy smoker, maybe five or six a day, so I didn't feel I was particularly bad for doing that.'

Amy said she felt that her and her mum's 'lived experience' might resonate with people. 'I'm not a professional, preaching,' she said, 'I'm just an ordinary person.'

She said: 'I got to the age of 12 and my gran would put a rollie down to go to the bathroom and I'd have a drag on it. It became so normal, but it's an addiction at the end of the day.

'Mum tried to stop smoking many times but it was always without any support. Having that support from the Stop Smoking campaign, the nicotine patches, the vapes, has made it so much easier – I quit with vapes but I think it's important to say they are not replacements for cigarettes, they are to help you stop.'

Amy said she felt brighter and had 'so much more energy' and enjoyed the taste of food more as a result of stopping smoking – and she has also saved money towards baby

things and for herself. 'Almost a year on I've saved so much money – I'm not getting to the end of the month and having to say no to things.'

Wendy added: 'I'm so proud of her and it's great that my grandchild will be brought up in a smoke-free environment – they won't see smoking as normal like I did.'

Turn the Corner is a collaborative campaign being co-ordinated by the Centre for Excellence in conjunction with all 15 local authorities across Yorkshire and Humber and Yorkshire Cancer Research, who are committed to reducing smoking and protecting local communities from the harms of tobacco. Scott Crosby, associate director of Centre for Excellence, said: 'Everyone knows someone who has been affected by tobacco harm.

'Smoking is the biggest cause of preventable death and ill-health in Yorkshire and Humber. It's a leading cause of health inequalities in the region and has a huge impact on people's lives.

'Every cigarette steals on average 20 minutes of life – that's why campaigns like 'Turn the Corner' are so important to raise awareness of the harm caused by tobacco. Wendy and Amy know first-hand the devastation that smoking has on your health and are a perfect example of how quitting can help you turn a corner.'

Tony Graham, director of retail, services and operations at Yorkshire Cancer Research, said: 'It's well known that smoking is strongly linked to lung cancer, but it is also a cause of at least 15 other types of cancer. As well as kidney cancer, smoking can lead to cancers of the mouth, throat, oesophagus, bladder, liver, pancreas, stomach, bowel, ovary, cervix, breast and, in some cases, even leukaemia.

'It remains the biggest preventable cause of cancer worldwide, and its impact can often span generations when children grow up seeing smoking as part of everyday life. Wendy and Amy's experiences show both the profound harm caused by tobacco and the powerful difference that quitting can make, not only for an individual's health, but for the health and future of their family.

'Even after a cancer diagnosis, stopping smoking can significantly improve how well treatments work, support better recovery, increase the likelihood of survival and reduce the risk of cancer coming back. By standing alongside our partners in this campaign, we hope more people across Yorkshire and Humber will feel supported and encouraged to take a step towards a longer, healthier life.'

8 April 2026

Why Support Matters

Explain why Wendy and Amy found it easier to quit with support rather than alone. Include different stop-smoking services methods, and one reason why getting help can make quitting feel more achievable.

Analysing Lived Experience

Amy says she is 'not a professional, preaching' but 'just an ordinary person'. Explain why lived experience can be powerful in a public health campaign. Then decide whether personal stories or health statistics are more persuasive, using evidence from the article.

Useful Websites

Useful websites

www.cancerresearchuk.org

www.exposetobacco.org

www.hulldailymail.co.uk

www.independent.co.uk

www.makesmokinghistory.co.uk

www.medicalnewstoday.com

www.news-decoder.com

www.nhs.uk

www.standard.co.uk

www.talktofrank.com

www.telegraph.co.uk

www.theconversation.com

www.tobaccoatlas.org

Further Reading

Pages 34-36: Web content: Cancer Research UK, https://www.cancerresearchuk.org/about-cancer/causes-of-cancer/smoking-and-cancer/how-do-i-stop-smoking, Accessed March 2026.

Books

Non-fiction

Tobacco and Smoking edited by Roman Espejo. Recommended age: 14+. This collection explores different viewpoints on tobacco use, health risks, alternatives to smoking and government regulation.

Fiction

The Perks of Being a Wallflower by Stephen Chbosky. Recommended age: 15+. This novel follows a teenager navigating friendship, trauma and identity, with scenes involving smoking, alcohol and drug use that require mature discussion.

Films, TV, or Documentaries

Addiction Incorporated (PG, 2011). This documentary follows scientist Victor DeNoble and his work exposing evidence about nicotine addiction within the tobacco industry.

The Insider (BBFC 15, 1999). This drama tells the story of a tobacco industry whistleblower and a journalist investigating corporate secrecy and public health.

Merchants of Doubt (PG-13, 2014). This documentary examines how public relations tactics, including those linked to the tobacco industry, have been used to cast doubt on scientific evidence.

Thank You for Smoking (BBFC 15, 2005). This satirical film follows a tobacco lobbyist and can be used to discuss persuasion, media spin and the ethics of marketing harmful products.

Disclaimer: Some of these titles include challenging themes linked to smoking, addiction, illness, peer pressure, grief, trauma or substance use, and may not be suitable for all readers or viewers. Students should speak to a parent or carer, teacher, or librarian if they are unsure whether a title is appropriate for them.

Glossary

Acetone
A colourless liquid used as a solvent, for example in nail polish remover. It is also found in cigarette and cigar smoke, and in some e-cigarette vapours.

Addiction
A strong need to keep using a substance or doing an activity, even when it causes harm. It may involve cravings, dependence, and difficulty stopping.

Ammonia
A chemical with a strong smell, used in cleaning products and fertilisers. It is also found in cigarette and cigar smoke, and in some vaping products.

Arsenic
A toxic substance used in some pesticides and found naturally in the environment. It is also present in cigarette and cigar smoke, and sometimes in vapour.

Cadmium
A toxic metal used in batteries and other products. It is also found in cigarette and cigar smoke and can build up in the body over time.

Cancer
A group of diseases where abnormal cells grow uncontrollably and may spread. Smoking and alcohol are major causes of many cancers.

Carbon monoxide
A colourless, odourless gas produced when fuels burn without enough oxygen. It is found in cigarette and cigar smoke and reduces oxygen in the blood.

Cigar
A roll of tobacco wrapped in a tobacco leaf, usually larger than a cigarette. It produces smoke that contains harmful chemicals.

Cigarette
A small roll of tobacco wrapped in paper that is lit and inhaled. It produces smoke containing many harmful substances.

Cigarillo
A small, narrow cigar, often without a filter. It is smoked in a similar way to cigarettes and produces harmful smoke.

Craving
A strong urge or desire to use a substance or repeat a behaviour, often linked to addiction.

Cyanide
A highly poisonous chemical that interferes with the body's ability to use oxygen. It is found in cigarette and cigar smoke.

Formaldehyde
A chemical used in building materials and preservation. It is also found in cigarette and cigar smoke, and in some vapours.

Heart disease
Conditions affecting the heart and blood vessels, increasing the risk of heart attacks and strokes.

Lung disease
Conditions that affect breathing, such as asthma or chronic obstructive pulmonary disease (COPD).

Nicotine
A chemical found in certain plants. It is present in tobacco products and many e-cigarettes and can lead to dependence.

Nicotine replacement therapy (NRT)
Products that provide small amounts of nicotine to help reduce cravings when stopping tobacco use.

Passive smoking
Breathing in smoke from other people's tobacco use. It can harm health even if you do not smoke.

Peer pressure
Influence from others that can affect a person's choices or behaviour.

Pipe smoking
Smoking tobacco using a pipe. The tobacco is burned in a bowl and the smoke is inhaled or puffed, exposing the user to harmful substances.

Quitting
The process of stopping a habit, especially one linked to dependence.

Secondhand smoke
Another term for passive smoking, referring to smoke breathed in from others' tobacco use.

Smoking
The act of inhaling and exhaling smoke from burning substances, often tobacco.

Smoking ban
A law that restricts smoking to protect people from harmful smoke. Smoking is banned in all enclosed public spaces and workplaces across the UK, introduced in 2007 (2006 in Scotland). New laws aim to create a 'smoke-free generation' by banning cigarette sales to people born on or after 1 January 2009 and may extend restrictions to some outdoor spaces.

Tar
A sticky mixture of chemicals produced when substances burn. It is found in cigarette and cigar smoke and can damage the lungs.

Third-hand smoke
Harmful chemicals left on surfaces and clothing after smoking has taken place.

Tobacco
A plant whose leaves are processed and used in products that are smoked, chewed, or inhaled.

Tobacco duty
A tax added to the price of tobacco products to reduce use and raise government revenue.

Vaping
Inhaling vapour produced by heating a liquid in a device such as an e-cigarette.

Withdrawal
Physical or mental symptoms that occur when a person reduces or stops using an addictive substance.

Index